Edited and with a Foreword
by Lawrence Harbison

MONOLOGUE AND SCENE STUDY SERIES

A SMITH AND KRAUS BOOK
HANOVER, NEW HAMPSHIRE

SMITHANDKRAUS.COM

Published by Smith and Kraus, Inc.
177 Lyme Road, Hanover, NH 03755
SmithandKraus.com

First Edition: September 2010
10 9 8 7 6 5 4 3 2 1

Cover design by Dan Mehling, dmehling@gmail.com
Book design and production by Julia Hill Gignoux,
Freedom Hill Design and Book Production

The Scene Study Series 1067-3253
ISBN-13 978-1-57525-773-0 / ISBN-10 1-57525-773-4
Library of Congress Control Number: 2010931855

NOTE: These scenes are intended to be used for audition and class study; permission is not required to use the material for those purposes. However, if there is a paid performance of any of the scenes included in this book, please refer to Rights and Permissions pages 171–176 to locate the source that can grant permission for public performance.

CONTENTS

SCENES

Foreword

This year Smith and Kraus Publishers has again combined its annual best monologues and best scenes anthologies. Here, you will find a rich and varied selection of monologues and scenes from plays that were produced and/or published in the 2009–2010 theatrical season. Most are for younger performers (teens through thirties), but there are also some excellent pieces for men in their forties and fifties, and even a few for older performers. Some are comic (laughs), some are dramatic (generally, no laughs). Some are rather short, some are rather long. All represent the best in contemporary playwriting.

Several of the monologues are by playwrights whose work may be familiar to you, such as Don Nigro, Theresa Rebeck, Craig Lucas, David Ives, and Craig Wright; others are by exciting up-and-comers like Christine Evans, Martin Blank, Shawn Nacol, Rachel Axler, Justin Warner, and Lisa Dillman. The scenes are by master playwrights, such as Theresa Rebeck and Terrence McNally, and by exciting new writers, such as Qui Nguyen, Maura Campbell, Henry Meyerson, Geoffrey Nauffts, and Daniel Talbot. All are representative of the best of contemporary writing for the stage.

Most of the plays from which these monologues have been culled have been published and, hence, are readily available either from the publisher, licensor, or a theatrical bookstore such as Drama Book Shop in New York. A few plays may not be published for a while, in which case contact the author or his or her agent to request a copy of the entire text of the play that contains the monologue that suits your fancy. Information on publishers and rights holders may be found in the rights and permissions section in the back of this anthology.

Break a leg in that audition! Knock 'em dead in class!

Lawrence Harbison
Brooklyn, New York

MONOLOGUES

AMERICAN WHUP-ASS

Justin Warner

More information on this playwright may be found in the "Meet Our Authors" tab at www.smithandkraus.com.

Comic
Corporal X, forties

Corporal X has been recruited during a very nasty Senate campaign to speak out against the current front-runner, a retired wrestler named General Mayhem.

CORPORAL X: *(Utterly serious and deeply ashamed.)* I served with General Mayhem in Dominica, in the 192nd Amphibious Division. Of course back then he wasn't General Mayhem, he was Private Stuart Littlecock. We were down there in the jungle . . . without any kind of modern amenities . . . just a bunch of guys out there in the wild. No moral supervision of any kind. And it was war, and we did what we had to do, you know, to take care of our basic needs . . .

(He pauses and dry heaves.)

Sorry. I'm having a really rough week with my chemo . . . so anyway, one night, we had all had a lot to drink, and Private Littlecock — he had a rather large . . . bowel movement . . . and we didn't have any paper, of course, and there were rumors that the jungle plants would give you a nasty rash. Which I myself learned the hard way. But Private Littlecock . . . he said he really needed to clean up, and he tore a piece off the flag on the company jeep . . . and he . . . *(Still traumatized.)* . . . wiped himself with it. He wiped his . . . anal area . . . with the American flag. I was the only one who saw it, and he swore me to secrecy, and I've kept that secret all this time, and I'm convinced that it's the reason I have cancer. Because it's been eating me up from the inside. So before I die, I just want the people of Nevada to know the truth. I wouldn't want a guy like that in the Senate. They have a lot of flags in those government buildings; they can't possibly keep track of them all . . .

AMERICAN WHUP-ASS

Justin Warner

Comic
Mayhem, forties

General Mayhem, a former professional wrestler, has been running a successful Senate campaign against well-meaning incumbent Wayne Kight: He challenged Senator Kight to a wrestling match, and when Kight didn't accept the challenge, his polls dropped. Kight then asked his campaign manager to take out Mayhem by any means necessary. The campaign manager digs up an unverifiable story that Mayhem, as a young soldier, once wiped his butt with the American flag, and a media frenzy ensues. But Kight soon regrets his actions and appears on national television with Mayhem to apologize and retract the accusation. He then gives Mayhem the chance to speak directly to the American people.

MAYHEM: Thanks, Senator. I appreciate your attempt to defend my character. But the fact is I don't need your charity. These allegations were cheap and uncalled for, they're none of anybody's business — but I'm not going to lie to you, America: they're true. Like the Corporal said, out in the jungle, you make do with what you got — decorum be damned. Now you all know what happens if you take a dump without finishing the wipe job. You chafe. You itch. You want to scratch it, pick at it, scrape your butt-crack against any available rough surface just to get one blessed moment of sweet relief. You can barely even think about anything else. What do you think happens if you do that in a war zone? You reach down to scratch your ass for even a split second and POW! There goes your hand! A sniper in the tree just shot it off! You try to stop the bleeding and BAM! There goes your head! And your buddy's standing next to you, slack-jawed, looking at your spurting bloody stump of a neck and then — RATATAT TAT! He's down! Jonesey's down! Smitty's down! They're picking you off like clay pigeons! There goes the company, the battle, the war, the whole frickin' civilized world!!! *I wiped my ass with that flag to save everything it stands for!* And anyone who doesn't understand that doesn't know what it really takes to defend America!

AMERICAN WHUP-ASS

Justin Warner

Comic

Corliss, sixties

A few months ago, Leslie Corliss, sixties, an unabashed corporate shill, looked like a shoo-in to unseat Nevada Senator Wayne Kight. But a showboating wrestler named General Mayhem steals his thunder and nearly walks away with the election by challenging Kight to a wrestling match. However, Kight's daughter Valerie runs against him in disgust, and after the wrestling match turns uglier than expected, the public throws its support behind Valerie. Because Valerie is too young to actually be elected senator, Corliss wins by default. Here, he addresses the people of Nevada in his victory speech.

CORLISS: People of Nevada. It's been a long, tough night, but I'm happy to accept the solemn responsibility you've given me this evening. I know that many, indeed most, of you did not actually cast your vote for me, but rather for a precocious little girl who isn't old enough to order a cosmopolitan, much less serve in the Senate. I also know that the outcome of this election will leave many of you disappointed, frustrated, even angry. Well, tonight, I'm here to tell you to go fuck yourselves. You hear that, people of Nevada? Screw you. Screw you all. You jerk me around through this whole ridiculous election, then you pass me over for some underage piece of ass, and now you expect me to spend the next six years trying to win your bloated, plaque-encrusted hearts? Think again, you yammering chorus of retarded monkeys. I loathe every single one of you! And I'm going to spend the next six years rewarding the only supporters I could ever really count on: great big corporations with shitloads of cash. Oh yes. We'll dump that toxic waste in your baby's bathtub if we feel like it. You want to complain? Don't bother calling my constituent relations line, because I'm disconnecting it. Go ahead and vote me out in six years, I don't care! I can do all I need to do in half that time. And when I get out, I'm going to retire to a fifty-acre villa in Monaco with the billions of dollars in kickbacks I rake in from my corporate cronies while you and your pathetic, squalling little children waste away from terminal brain cancer. Thank you, and God bless America!

CELL
Judy Klass

Dramatic
Byron, fifties

Byron, an African-American man, answers the probing questions of Dennis, the preppy, timid, white, much younger brother of Byron's friend Michael, whom Byron knows from their days living in a tent city in Tompkins Square Park.

BYRON: You're thinking how does a smart, charming man like myself get homeless? Now, that's an interesting question. How does one man's life hit the fan? But I'm not sure you're exactly the right guy to hear the answer. You understand, Dennis? I'm not sure you could really "identify." And it might mess up this image your brother is giving you about me, that I help the stray cats and little girls that wander into the park.
(Pause.)

I was married. I had a wife and a kid. A nice apartment. You'd be surprised. A good life. Some ignorant people think: you're born homeless, you've never lived on the other side. But plenty of guys live in society, go along thinking it's gonna be like that forever. Then, bam, it's all gone. Just like that. Damn, I had a thirty-inch TV, a sound system I was proud of. And I had a beautiful wife.
(Pause.)

And I loved that woman. Jesus. I never loved nobody that much, and I would have been right there for her till the day I died or she died, I would have been right there. And then I lose my job. And right away, I can see her respect for me going down. She couldn't even *see* me. I loved her for *her*, you understand what I am saying? Her love just start draining out of her, soon as I lose my job. She start seeing me as less than a man. And talking nasty about me to the kid, in this nasty tone of voice. And I go away with my buddies for a few days. Guy has a basement apartment, he's showin' kung fu movies, we just drunk and stupid, hangin' out for a weekend, nobody got a job, daddy Bush's recession, who the fuck cares, relax with the fellas for a little while. I get home. There is another man in the apartment with her. Another man sleeping with my wife — and maybe that was nothing new, and I was just blind before. But another man is in my home now, playing with my child. And my wife tells me the lease is in her name, I don't live there no more, she want a divorce, I should just take my things and go back to my friend's place.

(He pauses, remembering.)

My wife had a beautiful smile, and she knew it, too. A mouth full of pearly white, perfect teeth. A Colgate smile. You'd think she was smiling to be warm, or 'cause she like you — she just showing off those teeth. Make fun of me with my yellow teeth. So, I take a look at her, and this piece of shit man she got living in my house all of a sudden, and I knock some of those beautiful teeth right out of her smile. And I mess up his smooth face, and break a couple of bones, and they press charges, and I ain't got no lawyer worth a damn. And I do some time, and then when I get out, I wind up in the park. With a bunch of other losers without a life. Who threw it away, or had it taken away. A place your brother used to call . . . The Island of Lost Boys.

I had found a country that felt right to me, where I could belong. And when they closed down that country, I found me a subway train of my choice, and when they kick me off the train and it just get too cold, I wind up in the shelter. I been back to prison a few times, I don't mind it so much. I work out when I'm there, I get into shape. But the shelter ain't no place to be if you can help it. Does that answer your question?

CELL
Judy Klass

Dramatic
Dennis, early forties

Dennis is arguing with his brilliant, drug-damaged brother Michael, who is eleven years older.

DENNIS: *(Angry, near tears.)* You know, it's perfect that you equate persistence with a lack of imagination. Since you have never finished *one* thing you've started, in your entire life. How many unfinished stories, and novels, and experiments? How many causes and religions did you try on? What are you gonna be this week, Mike? An astronaut? A fireman? And whatever your theory or the project of the moment was, how *proud* Mom and Dad were! How full of hope, how *sure* you'd succeed! And then you'd flake out, drop out, and break their hearts again, kick them in the teeth again when they begged you to follow through.
(Furious.)

When you experimented on yourself and cooked your brain with every goddamned chemical you could get your hands on, with a new personality every week, they were the ones who really suffered. Just like your spaced-out, groovy friends made their families suffer. And I just sat on the sidelines and watched. And when the bunch of you were done being Kerouac or Peter Fonda or Timothy Leary or Jane Fonda, so many of you Boomers — not you, of course — settled down and became conservative yuppie scum. Still feeling righteous and somehow bohemian and daring all the while. You, on the other hand, just became an apolitical bum. But I watched it all happen, and I was not impressed. The bunch of you just feel so damn special, like whatever age you are, you're the first, you're the best — when it's just that there are *more* of you, so advertisers cater to you, all the films about young people when I was growing up had to be set in the fifties or sixties, except for putrid John Hughes films, otherwise we were invisible . . . Anyway. Whatever. Now you know what my issues are.

DEFENDER OF THE FAITH

Stuart Carolan

Dramatic
Thomas, twenty

Thomas's family is under suspicion. The IRA thinks there might be an informer in their midst. Here, Thomas talks with a farmhand, Barney, about the death of his brother Seamus.

THOMAS: All the time, Barney. All the time. I think about him all the time. Every day. Sure, it's only been a year. There was only a year and a half between us. Barney. Fourteen months. . . .

But I thought of him I suppose like a child. . . .

I know. The worst thing is I can look at him in the picture but I can't picture him in my head . . . And sometimes I have dreams where I see him getting shot in the dreams or somebody's tellin' me he's dead. Coming up to the backdoor of the house and saying your brother Shamey's been shot. And I'm going sweet God no, please no, no, please God, let him be OK. You can get shot and survive. He'll be all right. He's not dead. And the person's saying, it's too late, Shamey's dead. He's dead. And I'm saying no, no way, this is my worst nightmare. Shamey's dead and then just like that, Shamey walks in the door and says what's all the fuss about boy, and I'm thinking thank you God, thank you God, Shamey's all right. He's not dead. And then I'm happy like I've never been happy and then, and then, then I wake up. And for the first couple of minutes I'm happy. I'm still half asleep and I'm thinking Jasus, that was some nightmare that was. Shamey dead. Jasus. I must tell Shamey I had this nightmare where I thought he was dead. . . . And then I wake up proper and I remember he *is* dead. He's cold and he's in the ground. Shamey is dead and I can't go and tell him about my dream. Shamey is dead.

DEFENDER OF THE FAITH
Stuart Carolan

Dramatic
Thomas, twenty

Thomas is expressing his grief to his little brother Danny over the death of their brother Seamus.

THOMAS: Do you not want to see your mother? . . .

She'll be home soon I think. The last time I was up there, doctor said the new tablets were working much better. She'll be back home with us in no time. . . .

Oh, that's right she'll be back home to us soon enough. When will she be back, says you? Soon, says I. How soon says you? Oh soon enough, soon enough. Soon enough is right. The mother will be back. Back where she belongs. And then we'll all be together again. . . . And we'll all be fine.

Shamey. You and me and Danny and Mammy. We'll all be fine . . . Only we're not fine are we, Shamey? I'm not fine. No, not by a long shot.

So where's God in all of this Shamey? My brother Shamey. My brother. My brother is dead. My dead brother. Dead brother. Dead. Died. Two years since my brother died.

Are you a ghost now, Shamey? Is your spirit wandering around the place unhappy and sad, not knowing who it is? Faint memories of who you used to be and the people who loved you. Because I loved you, Shamey. I loved you and if you're a ghost or a spirit who forgot that once you used to be my brother . . . Shamey, then wake up! That's who you are, my brother, my brother Shamey, that I love. Spirit can you hear me? You are my brother Shamey. Tommy's brother Shamey that he loves.

When you died, Shamey, I would take your clothes and bury my head in them and close my eyes to catch the smell of you. Like the footprints of a ghost. Hold on to your T-shirt like a sick baby's sucky blanket. And furrow my brow so I looked like you and looking back in the mirror it was almost you, a ghost of you. A trace of you. You, my brother, my dear gentle dead brother. Tommy loves his brother.

DRIVING GREEN

Martin Blank

More information on this playwright may be found in the "Meet Our Authors" tab at www.smithandkraus.com.

Seriocomic
Tom, thirties

Tom is a disgruntled husband and employee of big oil. He is stuck in heavy traffic with his wife, Beth, a liberal employee of a save-the-environment nonprofit organization. The married couple struggle to survive their morning commute without killing each other. At this point, Tom has had enough.

TOM: You and your limousine liberal vegan friends, who preach tolerance, but won't tolerate an opinion other than their own. Trust-fund twits bragging about investing in socially conscience mutual funds when they own stock in Exxon Mobil, buying green houses and driving sport utility vehicles. Balding husbands in painted tans, with multiple face-lifts. Their wives drinking spinach smoothies, sitting around solar-heated swimming pools, with silicon breast implants, a nonbiodegradable product, made by Dow Chemical, the company which brought you napalm. With vegetarian teenage children sneaking McDonald's cheeseburgers, collecting money for Greenpeace, secretly hoping it will get them into Vassar. The family sitting around the dinner table eating pumpernickel bread, carrots, and turnips they found while dumpster diving, droning on about T. Boone Pickens and his plan. I say screw 'em. I want my meat cooked on a charcoal grill, rare. I want to drive a sixties muscle car, and when I floor it I can see the needle on the fuel gauge go down, down, down. I say live and live now. Because there's a good chance some crazy we pissed off at Gitmo is going to get his hands on a biological weapon or a dirty nuke and use it.

EMILIE'S VOLTAIRE
Arthur Giron

Dramatic
Voltaire, thirty-eight

It is 1733, in Paris. Voltaire and Emilie du Chatelet are being pursued by the queen's guards: she, because she owes the queen money; he, because he insulted an aristocrat. He is not an aristocrat, as she is, but is a wealthy poet, playwright, and businessman, who introduced coffee to Paris. Yet love has eluded him. Now, he has fallen madly in love with Emilie, who is gorgeous and his intellectual equal, yet his integrity is such that he tells Emilie that being with him could put her in mortal danger. By telling her the truth, he could lose her.

VOLTAIRE: Life isn't a matter of winning or losing where women and men are concerned. No, I am not gambling. I believe that we meet the correct person for us once in a life, maybe twice. I am not speaking of the numerous encounters we enjoy, but the chance of going beyond experimentation. It is important to embrace a discovery and not let that delight disappear. It is not true that there are countless women in the world who would fulfill me at some future time. I know enough to identify an actual woman. You. But . . . I must risk losing you, now that I have found you. I may be a commoner, a dishonorable pig, but my personal honor and love of truth compels me to warn you at this moment that if you become associated with me you will become known to the chief of police as the friend of a subversive man. Your friends at court will not protect you. The danger to your person is real. You have been protected all your life and assume that France is the zenith of civilization. No. Barely beneath the skin of our pride in oh-so-pretty achievements lies a barbaric disregard for the common man. Opposition — being different in any way — marks a man — or a woman — as an enemy. The weight of the crown strikes suddenly and without mercy. Madame, you are in mortal danger simply by being inquisitive. Your nature condemns you. Already you hide your intellectual labors in the countryside. But, your peace, I warn you, will be shattered by having my presence close by.

EMOTION MEMORY
Don Nigro

Seriocomic
Chekhov, thirty-six

Anton Chekhov has been out walking in the cold all night after the disastrous first performance of his play The Seagull *at the Maly Theatre. His friend Lyka, who's in love with him and who has been the model for the character of Nina in the play, has been waiting up for him all night, very worried. She's just asked him if he doesn't think the performance went well.*

CHEKHOV: It was a monstrous obscenity. The theater is a monstrous obscenity. It's an obscene, criminal activity. I tried to tell them to play it naturally, like life. I told them again and again. But the simpleminded jackasses just smiled and nodded their empty heads and ignored me. Poor fool, they said to each other. He's just a playwright. He knows nothing about the theater. Arrogant cretins. Even in my worst nightmares I could not have imagined what a grotesque abortion they made of my play. People in the audience were jabbering at each other during the performance, turning their backs to the stage, jeering so loud you couldn't hear the actors, and maybe it's just as well, because the actors were totally incompetent. The audience was moronic, and the critics are cannibalistic orangutans. I am lectured to about how to write by lip-diddling slugs who can barely scrawl their own names. The whole thing was like a scene from hell, with monkeys jumping up and down, hurling handfuls of excrement. This is what it is to be a playwright — to be urinated on by satanic monkeys. If I am ever stupid enough to write another play again, please do me the kindness of getting a gun and shooting me in the head.

When I was walking, what kept coming into my head was the night my brother died. I sat in the rain, waiting for seven hours for a train to come, in absolute despair, listening to some actors rehearsing some foolish melodrama on the other side of a wall. And it seemed to me that all of my life was plays within plays. Everybody is listening on the other side of a wall to some melodrama which is actually somebody else's life. The plays are all interconnected. The minor characters in the play of your life are major characters in their own plays. And one by one the plays come to an end, and the actors leave the stage, and then somebody else's play runs for a while, and it goes on until the sun explodes, and then what did it all mean? But while the play was being rehearsed, at least, there was something to give one's attention to. There was some value in that. But I was wrong. There is nothing in the world that can justify sitting in a theater and watching everything that's most precious to you shat upon by malicious cretins. Never again. Never, never again.

EMOTION MEMORY

Don Nigro

Seriocomic
Stanislavsky, thirty-five

Constantin Stanislavsky and the Moscow Art Theatre have done a very successful production of Chekhov's The Seagull, *and they have just given a performance in Yalta for Chekhov, who was unable to be at the opening. Chekhov, however, is horrified by what they've done, convinced that they've totally misunderstood his play and just done it badly in a different way from the disastrous earlier production. Stanislavsky has just asked Chekhov why, if it was so bad, did the audience clap until their hands bled, and Chekhov admits that he doesn't know, that it makes no sense to him. Stanislavsky, a tall, impressive-looking character actor, is desperate to convince Chekhov not to shut the production down.*

STANISLAVSKY: But that's the thing. It makes no sense. The theater never makes any sense. One night you're a genius, and the next night you're a fool. You think you've played well and they hate it. You think you've played badly and they love it. You do a great play and they despise it. You do a terrible play and they adore it. You're brilliant one night, you think you're doing it exactly the same way the next night, and suddenly they hate you again. You can work ten years on a part and still not understand it. You can understand it with your head and your body won't cooperate. You can know how to move and not have a clue how to speak. You open your mouth and the wrong words come out. You think the audience is hopelessly stupid and then suddenly they see things you didn't. You think they're smarter than you thought, and then they miss something so obvious a cow would understand it. You work like a dog and then the sofa catches fire or somebody in the first row vomits on your shoes. They pay people to write horrible things about you in the papers, people who in their whole life have never created anything but turds. It's absolutely maddening. You never get to the bottom of it. I could spend the rest of my life doing Uncle Vanya and still there'd be more to it that I hadn't discovered and also that you haven't discovered. It is utterly trivial work. And it is the most important thing I could possibly be doing.

It's somehow the key to the entire mad universe. It's investigating the inside of God's brain. It's everything. And if somehow, once in a while, one manages to do good work, despite everything, that is a very precious gift from out of the lunatic toy chest of time and chance, and you mustn't take this away from us. You can't. All right. It's true I didn't appreciate your play at first. Maybe I don't understand it yet. Maybe I just did a wonderful production of a play I don't understand at all. But something happened out there. We might not have found all the truth in it, but we found some of it. And the audience knew it. Each time we perform it, we'll find some more. Because your plays are like that. At first, they don't look like much. But once you get inside them, they prey upon your mind, and you can't get rid of them. They have rooms in them that keep opening up into other rooms. It's the most extraordinary thing. I don't know how you do it, and probably you don't know, either. But I do know that I want to spend the rest of my life living inside your plays. Nobody else in the history of the world will ever do your work with the love and attention and obsession that I will devote to them. If there are things I can't see now, I'll find them later. My mistakes will be more interesting than other people's triumphs. I'll get on my knees and beg you if I have to. Don't take this away from me.

FARRAGUT NORTH

Beau Willimon

More information on this playwright may be found in the "Meet Our Authors" tab at www.smithandkraus.com.

Dramatic
Tom, forties to fifties

Tom is a hard-boiled political campaign manager. He is giving some words of advice to Steve, press secretary for a governor who is running for president. He thinks Steve is betting on the wrong horse.

TOM: You're a smart guy, Steve. Very smart. But there's a lot of smart guys out there. I've seen 'em rise and fall, and when they fall — they fall hard. Eventually they make a wrong move or get too arrogant or get too paranoid or just plain buckle under all the pressure. You know what I'm talking about. The heels at your back. Guys twice your age jealous of you. Younger guys circling like vultures. You start making enemies you don't even know you had. That's a terrible feeling, isn't? Constantly looking over your shoulder, wondering who you can trust. Always wondering who's gonna screw you next.

You've got something the other guys don't have. You've got a special . . . what is it? Charm isn't the right word. It's more than that. You *exude* something. You draw people in. All the reporters love you. Even the ones that hate you love you. You play them all like they're pieces on a chessboard. And you make it look effortless. We both know how much work it takes, constantly being on guard, weighing every word so carefully, every move. But from the outside, you make it look easy. People are scared of you because they don't understand how you do it, and they love you for it. There's nothing more valuable in this business — the ability to win people's respect by making them mistake their fear for love.

About twenty percent of what you think is your solid support is actually our people posing as Morris supporters. Inflates your lead, makes you feel comfortable, makes us look like the underdog. Three days ago we started telling them to switch back over to us when the pollsters call. During the next week, the tracks will show us gaining steadily and finally overtaking you a day or two before the caucus. It'll look like we've made a come-from-behind victory out of nowhere, when in reality we've had the lead all along. We'll have the momentum out of Iowa and take New Hampshire on the twenty-seventh. Morris will throw in the towel by Super Tuesday.

Our field director talks to a hundred organizers. Each of those organizers talks to a dozen precinct captains. The precinct captains call fifty, a hundred supporters they trust. Do the math, Steve. That's what — fifteen thousand voters at least. Over ten percent of the vote.

You really think I'd have you drive all the way out here to blow smoke up your ass. What good would it do me to show you these numbers if they weren't real? Take them. Have Morris hit every county in the state. You might pick up a point or two, but you don't have enough time to close the gap. I'm not showing you these numbers to try and intimidate you, Steve. I'm showing you these numbers because I want you to work for a winner. You're too good to work for a loser.

These numbers are just the tip of the iceberg. A week ago I brought three hundred more field staff to pump up the GOTV. We've got over six hundred organizers under the radar that nobody knows about. The day before the caucus we'll robo-call and mass mail the hell out of your supporters with wrong polling locations. On game day, I'll send vans out to your strong areas to cause traffic jams so your supporters can't get to their caucuses. And once everyone gets into the caucus room, you'll find that a third of your precinct captains are actually our people. And by the way — we've got Thompson in the bag.

We promised Thompson secretary of labor, so he'll do anything we tell him to do — like sticking a carrot in front of your noses until we tell him to yank it away. Iowa's already over, Steve. It's been over for weeks. I'm thinking way down the road now. That's why I want you. We need the best. I'll bring you in straight at the top.

What is it you love about your job? *(Beat.)* I bet I know. It's not about power. If you wanted power you'd work on Wall Street, or in Hollywood. And it's not about money, 'cause we both know this line of work doesn't pay. And it's definitely not any idealistic nonsense about making a difference. Otherwise, you'd slave away for Greenpeace or PETA or some other piece of crap nonprofit. You love your job because you know you're the best at what you do. It makes you feel invincible. But you still have one hurdle to jump. You want that desk with a window two doors down from the Oval Office with reporters poking in and hanging on your every word. You want that moment when you wake up next to your girlfriend at five in the morning, climb out of bed, make yourself a cup of coffee, and can think to yourself — I've made it. I'm at the height of my game. And in that moment the burning stone that's been lodged in your gut since you can remember — it will vanish. You'll know — without a shred of doubt in your mind — that you've made it so high there's nowhere higher left to go.

FARRAGUT NORTH
Beau Willimon

Dramatic
Paul, forties

Paul is the campaign manager for a governor who is running for president. He is telling Steve, the campaign's young press secretary, that he is firing him because he doesn't trust him.

PAUL: No Stephen. You didn't make a mistake. You made a choice. Yesterday — remember when you called me on the way to the airport? Remember that? "Hi Paul, this is Steve. I just got a . . . " What? What did you just get? A call from Duffy? No. That's not what you told me. You stopped yourself. You made up some bullshit to cover yourself. You *chose* Stephen. You *chose* not to tell me. Why did you make that choice? Because you were curious. Because you were flattered. Because it made you feel special to think Duffy wanted to speak to you instead of me. Because you thought to yourself: maybe I can get something out of this. Because it made you feel *big.*

(Paul takes out his wallet and pulls out a folded-up dollar bill.)

You know what this is? *(As he unfolds the bill.)* First campaign I ran — tiny little race in Kentucky — state senate seat. Workin for a redneck nobody named Sam McGuthrie. Had no money, no staff, no fuckin' office. Worked out of McGuthrie's garage. Everyone thought we didn't stand a chance. But sure enough, we start to turn things around. Our numbers go up. Donations start trickling in. We hire a few people. Rent an office. Next thing you know, Sam looks like he's got a real chance. Incumbent is running scared. So what happens? State Republican Party doesn't want to lose this seat. They pour fifty grand into the other guy's coffers. Doesn't seem like a lot to us now, but in a small race like that, twenty years ago? It was a fortune. There's no way we can compete. Our party decides to abandon Sam. Didn't want to spend the money for a seat they thought they were gonna lose anyway. And about this time, a guy running a congressional campaign a few districts over gives me a call. Says, "I really like what you were able to do for poor ole Sam. But let's face it, he's a goner, so why don't you come work for me?" What do

I do? Well Stephen — this is where you and I are different. I told Sam about the call. And Sam says to me, "Paul, you think this other guy's got a shot at winning, and he can pay you more than anything I can afford, so if it's what you feel you need to do, then I won't get in your way." So I say, "Sam — you took a chance and hired me when I was even more of nobody than you are, and I'd be damned if I'm gonna jump ship just because the shit hit the fan." We froze all the staff's salaries and poured every dime we had into winning the race. By election day, I was literally down to one dollar in my pocket. This dollar. *(He crumples up the dollar and tosses it to Stephen.)* We lost the race, but three years later, when Sam decided to run for governor — who do you think he called? We *won* that race. And twenty years later, I'm where I am now. *(Beat.)* There's only one thing I value in this world, Steve, and that's loyalty. Without it you're nothing and you have no one. And in politics it's the only currency that you can count on. That's why I'm letting you go. Not because you're not good enough. Hell, you're the best. But I value trust over skill. And I don't trust you anymore.

FROST/NIXON
Peter Morgan

Dramatic
Nixon, sixties

Former President Nixon has agreed to be interviewed by British television journalist David Frost. On the night before the two will be discussing the Watergate scandal, Nixon phones Frost to vent about how the two of them are more alike than Frost realizes. He is drunk, but fiercely determined to best what he believes to be a less-than-formidable adversary.

NIXON: Watergate. It's a small consolation to me that for the next couple of days, that word will be as much of a millstone around your neck as it has been around mine. Because I guess, the way you handle Watergate will determine whether these interviews are a success or failure. Should I be nervous?

You know, it's strange. We've sat in chairs opposite one another, talking for hours, it seems days on end . . . and yet I've hardly gotten to know you. One of my people . . . ah . . . as part of the preparation of this interview . . . did a profile of you, and I'm sorry to say . . . . I only got around to reading it tonight. There's some interesting stuff in there. The Methodist background, modest circumstances. Then off to a grand university. Full of richer, posher types. What was it? Oxford? . . .

Did the snobs there look down on you, too? . . .

Of course they did. That's our tragedy, isn't it, Mr. Frost? No matter how high we get, they still look down on us . . .

No matter how many awards — or how many column inches are written about you — or how high the elected office is for me — it still isn't enough, am I right? We still feel like the little man? The loser they told us we were? A hundred times. The smart-asses at college. The high-ups. The well-born. The people whose respect we really wanted. Really craved. And isn't that why we work so hard now? Why we fight for every inch? Scrambling our way up, in undignified fashion, whatever hillock or mountain it is, why we never tire, why we find energy or motivation when any sensible person would lie down, or relax. If we're honest for a minute. If we reflect privately just for a moment . . . if we allow ourselves . . . a glimpse into that shadowy place we call our soul, isn't that why we're here now . . . ? The two of us? Looking for a way back? Into the sun? Into the limelight? Back onto the winner's podium? Because we could feel it slipping away? We were headed, both of us, for the dirt. The place the snobs always told us we'd end up. Face in the dust. Humiliated all the more for having tried so pitifully hard. Well, to hell with that. We're not going to let that happen. Either of us. We're going to show those bums, and make them choke on our continued success. Our continued headlines. Our continued awards, power, and glory. We're going to make those motherfuckers choke. Am I right? . . .

Yes. And I shall be your fiercest adversary. I shall come at you with everything I've got. Because the limelight can only shine on ONE of us. And for the other, it'll be the wilderness. With nothing and no one for company, but those voices ringing in our heads. You can probably tell . . . I've had a drink. Not too many. Just one or two. But believe me, when I wake up tomorrow, I'll be focused and ready for battle. Well, good night, Mr. Frost.

FROST/NIXON
Peter Morgan

Dramatic
Frost, thirties

Former President Nixon has agreed to be interviewed by British television journalist David Frost. In this, the final segment of those historic interviews, Frost makes the bombshell revelation that Nixon's staff has uncovered clear evidence that Nixon was involved in the Watergate cover-up.

FROST: There's one conversation with Charles Colson in particular, which I don't think has ever been published. . . .

One of my researchers found it in Washington. Where it's available to anyone who consults the records. . . .

It's where you say . . . "This whole investigation rests unless one of the seven begins to talk. That's the problem." . . .

You've claimed you first learned of the break-in on June twenty-third. But this transcript clearly shows that to be a falsehood. And in a subsequent transcript of March twenty-first in one conversation alone, there in black and white, I picked out . . . and these are your words. *(Frost reads from a clipboard.) One,* "You could get a millions dollars and you could get it in cash. I know where it could be gotten." *Two,* "Your major guy to keep under control is Hunt." *Three,* "Don't we have to handle the Hunt situation?" *Four,* "Get the million bucks. It would seem to me that would be worthwhile." *Five,* "Don't you agree that you'd better get the Hunt thing going?" *Six,* "First you've got the Hunt problem. That ought to be handled." *Seven,* "The money can be provided. Ehrlichman could provide the way to deliver it. That could be done." *Eight,* "We've no choice with Hunt but the one hundred and twenty thousand dollars, or whatever it is, right?" *Nine,* "Christ, turn over any cash we've got." *(Frost looks up at Nixon.)* Now, it seems to me, that someone running a cover-up couldn't have expressed it more clearly than that. Could they?

THE GINGERBREAD HOUSE

Mark Shultz

More information on this playwright may be found in the "Meet Our Authors" tab at www.smithandkraus.com.

Dramatic
Brian, early to midthirties

Brian blames his children for his lack of success and for the lack of spark in his and Stacey's marriage. Here, he tells her that he wants to get rid of them. Wasn't life better without them? Weren't they happy?

BRIAN: *(Beat.)* I mean ask yourself. Honestly. Weren't we happier? Before? Didn't we do things? Didn't we go places? Didn't we have. Stacey. Fuck. Didn't we have friends? Fucking *friends.* Stacey? That we visited. And ate with. And. Weren't you. I mean don't you feel like. Weren't you prettier? Or happier? Or. I don't know. *I* think you were. I know *I* was. I mean. You were so much more. Beautiful. Just a few years ago. Remember? I couldn't even. I couldn't keep my fucking hands. Off of you. . . .

Yeah but now. Stace. Look at us. Gray hairs. And exhaustion. All the time. And when we fuck. *If* we fuck. If I can touch you. And I miss touching you. If I can touch you. It's like. It's like. It's just wrong. It's bad. And it's wrong. And. Perfunctory. And. Mechanical. And. We're like. It's like. Two. Corpses. Fucking. No future. No future. No fucking future. Everything lost. See it in the distance. Going. Going. Going. And gone. And gone. And. Gone.

(Beat.)

And you gotta ask. What's different? Right? What's different? Well. Stace. It's the kids. It's the kids. And. It's poison. It's poison. And it's bad. And it's wrong. And they need to go. And I can't look at them. I can't *look* at them. I can't. Be in the same *room.* Knowing. They swallowed it up. They took it and they swallowed it up. Our happiness. And I want it back. For us. For both of us.

(Beat.)

Don't you miss. Being happy?

THE GINGERBREAD HOUSE
Mark Shultz

Dramatic
Marco, early to midthirties

Marco, a friend of Brian's, moonlights as a child broker. Here, he is trying to convince Stacey to sell her children.

MARCO: Do you see that? Those trees? That gorgeous building? That huge. Gorgeous. Mansion. Building? Do you know what that is? . . .

That's where they're going. . . .

Yes. Exactly. Yes. Absolutely. Look at that. The lush countryside. Nestled amongst which: one of the finest examples. Of old-world European opulence.

(Beat.)

Stacey I'm gonna lay it all out. I represent. The interests. Of a very sad couple. A very sad. And desperate couple. Who happen to be. Fabulously wealthy. And who wish to remain. For the present. Anonymous. The source of their sadness? Can you guess? The wellspring of their woe? Stacey? They're barren. OK? They're barren. The one thing in life that could give them any joy. Any happiness. Is children. Many children. Which they themselves. Cannot produce. They've tried everything. Fertility pills. In vitro fertilization. Surrogates. Nothing. Ruin and disaster all of it. The emotional fatigue, Stacey. I don't think I need to tell you. Has made them desperate. They are willing. To do anything. For children. And they have put all the resources at their disposal. Into finding. The perfect kids. To complete their family.

THE GINGERBREAD HOUSE
Mark Shultz

Dramatic
Brian, early to midthirties

Brian and Stacey have sold their kids to Marco, a friend of Brian's who moonlights as a child broker. Stacey wants her kids back, but Marco refuses, so she has stolen Marco's kids in a desperate bid to get them back. Brian's tired of her intransigence and tired, too, of what he perceives to be Stacey's rejection of him in favor of the children they sold to buy a better life. Stacey's gone so far as to say that she can make it without him as long as she gets her kids back. Here, Brian levels with her and paints a picture of what life without him will really be like.

BRIAN: OK, I'm pretty fucking tired of this. Stacey? You know what? You wanna know what? You think you can get out of this you think you can leave? Then get the fuck out already. Just get the fuck out. Get out of my fucking house. And *out.* Of my fucking *life.* And you go. And live. Alone. Out there. With them. With your dead fucking kids.

With your greedy fucking hungry fucking dead ghost fucking children. You make a life with *them.* If you can. If "life." If the word "life" is any way to describe that sort of endless fucking misery. You try living with *them.* All. Alone. With your "pain." And your guilt. And your guilt. And your useless fucking gnawing fucking guilt. All. Alone. 'Cause I can't take it. I won't take it.

And if you realize one day you can't do it. That you can't *actually* live like that either. With them. Cold and hungry and crying and staring at you day in and day out with their cold hungry dead eyes. If one day you wake up and you realize you should have gotten rid of them *all* of them every *bit* of them every *thought* of them a long time ago when you had the chance. If you realize *that. When* you realize that. I hope you think of me. And I hope you think of us. Of what we had. Of what *you* lost. And I hope you see me happy. Full of all the happiness *you* rejected. Sharing it with someone happy. And grateful. And I hope you hear me laughing. Laughing laughing laughing. At *you.* Because I will *not* shed a tear. Not *one* tear. When that door closes behind you. And you vanish with the ghosts. That you loved. That you *insisted* on loving. More. Than me.

But hey. You know. Whatever. Fine. Do it your way. You wanna suffer? Go ahead. Suffer. You wanna feel horrible? You feel horrible. You *be* horrible. Tell you what: you *are* horrible. As a mother *or* a fucking vampire hag. And I take *no* responsibility for that. That's all you. You live with it. You sit with it. You be it. You *are* it. You have fun. That's *not* my world. And that's *not* my problem.

So good riddance. Is all I can say. Just give Marco back his kids already Stacey. And get the fuck out.

THE GOOD NEGRO
Tracey Scott Wilson

Dramatic
James, thirties

James is a civil-rights activist, modeled on Martin Luther King Jr. Here, he is talking about the time he was thrown in jail and about his unshakeable conviction that freedom is coming.

JAMES: When this first started. My second time in jail. They put me in a cell with some white inmates. I was terrified. They were beating me, threatening to lynch me. I just prayed. Lord Jesus, if I have to die let me die a man. Please don't let them cut me. And I'm praying hard because I know this is it. Then all of a sudden . . . This happens sometimes. When they beat you, you learn to tune it all out . . . the nigger this and nigger that. But all of a sudden I heard . . . It was like the Lord wanted me to hear how stupid they were so I wouldn't be scared. This one bucktoothed, cross-eyed man who's beating me is saying over and over "you ain't gonna marry my daughter, you ain't gonna marry my daughter." And it just hit me. Marry his daughter? Why would I want to marry his ugly assed daughter? . . . I started laughing. They must have thought I was crazy 'cause they stopped beating me. *(Pause.)* I felt such a peace then. Right there in the midst of all that craziness. I felt a peace 'cause I knew the Lord must be saving me for something. This is the something, Rutherford. I can see it. For the first time in a long time I can see it. Freedom. Freedom is coming.

GROUND
Lisa Dillman

Dramatic
Coop Daniels, early sixties

Coop, an industrial pecan grower and head of Citizens Alliance, the local civilian border defense group, is attempting to persuade Zelda Preston, the owner of another local farm, that a Citizens Alliance–built fence should seal off the back end of her property from illegal entry over the Mexican border.

COOP: Personally? I hate the idea of a border fence. I really do. My family did business with the Mexicans for decades, just like yours did. But get caught hiring them these days you're in a whole world of hurt. So, lookit: we can't work them, but they're still coming because the government won't seal this border. Which is why there's Citizens Alliance and the volunteer fence movement. You look confused.

Well. Last fall this particular farmer was robbed at gunpoint by illegals right here on his own land. Broad daylight. Happily for him, they didn't blow his head off. Next time he might not be so lucky. My opinion, a man shouldn't need that much "luck" on his own ground. This fence is funded by donations from thousands of concerned citizens across the country. I live here. I do all right. But I can't just sit by while illegals gobble up my community's social services and pave the way for the economic free fall of the industries along this border. Lookit, a federally funded wall from Texas to the Pacific, that would be great. And it might even happen one day. But until it does, we the people are gonna have to go one volunteer project at a time. Because let me ask you this, Zelda: Do you like for strangers to take money right out of your pocket? See the gal driving the Bobcat? She's an out-of-work nurse from Greeley. Lost her job because her hospital got so overrun with illegals it had to shut down. Third one in the state. These days the nearest hospital is three hours from Fronteras, did you know that? Nearest clinic's sixty-three miles. That gal look like a vigilante to you? Would you feel the same if she wasn't Latina? You don't need to answer that. But it might interest you to know that nearly a quarter of our membership is Latino. See, race doesn't matter to Citizens Alliance — that gal, like all of us out here, is simply an American protecting her home against further invasion. After all, what's more sacred than home and hearth, Zelda? You tell me.

GUINEA PIG SOLO

Brett C. Leonard

More information on this playwright may be found in the "Meet Our Authors" tab at www.smithandkraus.com.

Dramatic
José, late twenties to midthirties.

José is a New York–born Puerto Rican (Nuyorican) and an Iraq War veteran. He is a contemporary Woyzeck. His wife has taken out a restraining order against him. They have a young son. He is in a bar, speaking to his best friend, Gary, whom he has known since they were children in uptown New York.

JOSÉ: I don't give a shit about rats. I don't give a shit about elephants. I don't give a fuck about giraffes or turtles, zebras, two-headed snakes, or the hump-backed motherfuckin' whale! I don't fuckin' care about that shit! I got bigger fish ta fry, ya understand? Bigger fish. I DON'T GIVE A SHIT WHY SALMON SWIM UPSTREAM! Jesus fuckin' Christ!! YOU can talk about bullshit! You can try ta learn ta think of nothing if that's what you wanna do — just leave my shit out of it, OK? LEARN TA THINK OF NOTHING — shit doesn't even make any goddamn sense! Ya learn something — you learn SOME-THING! Not NO-THING! SOME-THING. You learn SOME-THING — fuckin' shit, bro! It's no way ta go through life thinkin' that shit, learnin' nothin', talkin' bullshit twenny-four seven. We are what we are — An' ya know what? We don't stand a chance, guys like you an' me — deck stacked up against us an' all that shit. The doctor with the welfare moms? The dentist from Bed-Stuy? I don't know those mothafuckers — you know those mothafuckers? How many Colin Powells we grow up playin' dodgeball with? Bullshit. Your father — he doin' twenny-five ta life he ran a little weed tryin' ta put food on the table, your moms is walkin' dead bustin' her ass sixteen-eighteen hours a day cleanin' toilets a' some silver-spoon bullshit — ya gettin' your ass ahead goin' through it that way? Ivy League diploma on your motherfuckin' wall next ta the crucifix an' the busted-up cockroach legs? Fuck that! Not in this world OR the next — if there even is a next — an' what is it you think about that shit? Huh?

Whaddayou think? There's a heaven, there's a God? Look around your ass — look out your window someday, ridin' subways, lookin' at the faces standin', sittin' all around you. If we're created in God's image, that's one sad, long-faced, all-powerful motherfucker. Shoulda made us in somebody else's image. Rich motherfucker's image. Rolex watches, penthouse apartments, cars an' private drivers — they piss on guys like you an' me. In their eyes they shit on us. We're on welfare an' food stamps an' park benches with newspaper blankets, pissin' our pants, panting for their daughters with eyes buggin' out our fuckin' heads — sittin' on the stoop drinkin' forties, taggin' their precious city-owned overpriced walls. Fuck George Senior! And George W. too! Dick Cheney — all them mothafuckers. Mayor Mike Bloomberg? Fuck him too. I wanna cigarette I'll smoke it wherever the fuck I feel like smokin' it. "An unattended cart is an unattended cart." "Don't blame me, blame Bloomberg." I blame all y'all mothafuckers. Thumbin' their coke-filled noses at guys like you an' me — howlin' at the moon — playin' with our switchblades — dirty Porta Rican spick-ass motherfuckers — messin' with their fire hydrants, wilding in the park. It's two hundred thirty seven degrees out, got no air conditionin', got no super ta fix 'em when we do got 'em — you goddamn right I'm fuckin' with the hydrants. I'll sit smack dead middle a that shit NAKED — water shootin' straight up my sweet brown Puerto Rican ass. I'll put a mothafuckin' MILK CRATE on top of the fuckin' hydrant, sit on that shit, an' I'll smoke me a mothafuckin' Newport while I'm at it! Fuck dem bitches! NYPD. USMC. They can all tongue my piss-hole all I care. It's our lot in LIFE — it'll be our lot in mothafuckin' DEATH. Be put ta work in Heaven if we're lucky enough ta get there in the first place. All of us — every last one — poor motherfuckers? You don't got no cash? Ain't put away 'nuff greenbacks your ass was on the earth? Get over there, bitches, get in the I-don't-got-no-motherfuckin' money line up in Heaven. Or the English-is-my-second-language line. Or the your-skin-ain't-quite-white-enough line — fuck you — all a you — over there against the wall, hands up an' spread 'em, this shit is mothafuckin' shake-down time. Be on Heaven's assembly line pullin' down minimum-fuckin' — I work at Burger King wages — makin' the thunder an' the lightning for niggas still living down below. An' other mothafuckers up there with us? Rich, white mothafuckers, got their hands in Wall Street? Got their hands in oil down in Texas? Be havin' orgies an' chill-ass Grey Goose apple-flavor martinis, kickin' with slot machines an' lucky sevens, filet mignons an'

French shit I can't even pronounce. Not us, bro. To the assembly lines. It's nine-eleven, an' December seven, an' the fourth of motherfuckin' July 1776. September eleven mighta woke up some niggas but it didn't wake up enough a them still sound sleepin' countin' sheep motherfuckers. Sleepin' hard. Sleepin' deep, bro. Smilin', peaceful, wakin' up in wet dreams an' silk sheets — I'm Afghanistan. Operation Iraqi Occupation. Vietnam. I'm the mothafuckin' beaches a Normandy. I waved my motherfuckin' flag. I was over there while bitches sat on their fat Twinkie eatin' asses tunin' in on motherfuckin' CNN, wishin' us well, wishin' us safe return. Blood and oil on my body, my clothes, my hair — in my motherfuckin' eyes — holding a three-year-old Iraqi girl's intestines in my hands, tryin' ta resuscitate her, she's already fuckin' dead. Her intestines in my hands. Go over there and kill, soldier. Go over there an' try ta stay alive so I can profit from your insanity. Make me rich, soldier, make me richer than I already am. Pat on the back, thank you for your troubles, good luck at the food stand, best a' luck at the barbershop. What's with the long face, soldier? Ya did good, soldier, put a smile on your face, soldier, walk proud, soldier, stand tall — and by the way — oh yeah — welcome back, soldier — welcome home — sure is glad ya didn't catch one in the gut while you were there, happy ya didn't get one to the head — sorry 'bout your buddies Tommy an' Luke an' Justin an' lil' Frankie — sorry they didn't make it, but yeah, boy, yessir, we sure is glad ta see you doin' all right — how about a ribbon? Would ya like a ribbon, soldier? How 'bout a medal or two you can wear while you're out sellin' hot dogs an' lemonade? Tha'd be nice, donchya think? Every second, every day they bleed me of my life, of my wife, of my child, of who I am myself. That which does not kill me makes me wanna kill somebody else. Kill or be killed? Love and be loved. To love and be loved — nothing else — nothing. Everything else is fuckin' bullshit — dogshit — catshit. Love and be loved. Or eat a fuckin' dick.

(Beat.)

I'm lyin'? Mmmph? I'm lyin'? C'mon, gimme another cigarette, bro. I don't wanna be late to my fuckin' RE-scheduled appointment.

GUINEA PIG SOLO
Brett C. Leonard

Seriocomic
Gary, thirties

Gary is speaking to his best friend, José, who has recently returned from fighting the war in Iraq. José is depressed, sleeps on Gary's couch, estranged from his wife and son. José's wife has taken out a restraining order against him. Gary is trying to cheer him up, get him to go out for a night on the town, find another woman and forget about his wife.

GARY: All right. All right. Listen, bro — all right? You know about Abraham Lincoln an' his wife? Mmmmph? You know about that shit? . . . No, no, no — no — listen ta this shit, all right? Honest Abe had this wife, all right — that he was married to. OK? This was the SECOND love of his life — the FIRST love of his life died when he was like nineteen or somethin'. Old Abe had a tough time of it from what I understand. His first love died a' some tragic something-or-other, his mom's died when he was really young — lotta shit-fuckin' log cabin — but he had this wife he ended up gettin' married to, OK? And she was a midget. OK? A little fuckin' midget. And ol' Abe? This motherfucker was some'n like . . . six-five, six-six or some shit — a fuckin' giant, OK? Are you listening?

And thusly the reason for the restraining order in the first place. Now lemme finish my goddamn story, all right? Now listen carefully to this shit. OK. So — ol' Abe — Abraham fuckin' six-foot-six born-in-a-log-cabin motherfucker — this goofy-bearded motherfucker marries a midget woman no taller than this big — this fuckin' high she was — like a half a midget. And she useta beat the shit outta him. All right? The fuckin' midget would BEAT THE LIVIN' SHIT outta her husband — and what husband was that, José? Joe Blow? Ordinary Schmo? Guy like you or me? No! This was ABRAHAM LINCOLN. She'd beat the shit outta Abraham fuckin' Lincoln. The lil' midget. Fuckin' guy could free an entire peoples of the horrors of fuckin' slavery — he could not control his own lil' midget wife. That's all I'm sayin'. Now come on. It's ass time.

GUINEA PIG SOLO
Brett C. Leonard

Seriocomic
Charlie, sixties

Charlie is an Italian-American New York City cop and a Vietnam War vet. He is in a barbershop, giving advice on love to José, a young Puerto Rican New Yorker recently home from the Iraq War.

CHARLIE: I fell in love twice this morning, Joey. Look. You fall in love, whad does it mean? You'd take a bullet for her? She's all you think about? She makes your heart beat, makes your cock throb? It's all of the above. This morning, I step in a bodega — get my cigarettes — get my coffee — a wintergreen can of Altoids. Young girl — one a your kind — brown skin, brown eyes — beautiful — rings me up at the register. Couldn't a been more'n nineteen. Maybe twenny, twenny-one. I give her the money, she gives me a smile. What'm I thinkin' about? My phone bill? My fuckin' grandkids? I'm thinkin' about HER. Heart gets a little boom-boom-boom, activity begins stirring in the pants — and if some Dominican motherfucker had walked in there with a gun? I'd a stepped in front of her and taken one in the chest. In that moment. Ya understand? People get too, uh . . . all right Joey, I'm gonna tell ya somethin'. A little somethin' I know to be true about love. It's a moment-to-moment thing if you want it to be successful. Ya gotta say to yourself — yes — I am presently enjoying the company of this lovely young lady by my side. This . . . is a good time that I am having — and don't make more of it than what it is. Start thinkin' 'bout the future? Start shoppin' out his-and-hers cemetery plots? This is not love, Joey. This is a mistake of the delusional. You enjoy yourself. Ya take it as it comes. Ya grow a little paunch, get a touch a' gray, start payin' for sex. All a part a' God's great plan. This ETERNAL love crap, Joey. It's for the fuckin' birds.

A HUMAN INTEREST STORY (OR THE GORY DETAILS AND ALL)

Carlos Murillo

More information on this playwright may be found in the "Meet Our Authors" tab at www.smithandkraus.com.

Seriocomic
Anonymous Man, thirties

Anonymous Man's thirties have not been kind to him. He's unsuccessful both in work and in love and struggles to find the rudder that will get his life back on track. In this monologue, he speaks to unseen detectives, responding to questions about a brutal murder-suicide of a married couple he recently visited for a weekend. The intent of his visit — to restore his faith in relationships after breaking up with his girlfriend of five years — is thwarted when he learns of the rot underneath his friends' seemingly successful marriage. In this monologue, he begins his tale — navigating the pain and discomfort with the situation through humor and spinning the metaphor of the Crafty Baboon, a jungle animal with which he painfully identifies.

ANONYMOUS MAN: Did you catch that documentary they showed on Discovery Channel? *Baboon Warriors of the Serengeti?*

Man . . .
It was *fucked.*
up.

I saw it last Thursday night and I can't get the fucking thing out of my head. It was incredible, the whole thing was just un. b. *liev*able. I mean those little fuckers are *mean.*

There was this *one* part
And this, this is the part that really *stuck* with me
the part I can't extricate from my craw I mean
Jesus . . .
They were talking about this *thing*
this whole *phenomenon* that happens on planet baboon
this whole *phenomenon* of a certain *kind* of baboon they call

The *Crafty* Baboon

. . . see:

Baboons have a whole tribal hierarchy thing going

the alpha males hunt the food and fight the wars

beta males make this perimeter around the camp keeping watch so the *fe*males staying at home can rear little future alphas in *peace*. . . .

End of the day

Alphas come home from the hunt

and being all tired, sweaty, and riled up from the hard work

naturally

they're in the mood to *get* some

a kind of payment or reward or whatever

for busting their asses out in the jungle all day.

Simple . . .

But *then*

there's this *other* kind a baboon

The *Crafty* Baboon.

He's like the third or fourth string male

the dead weight

the useless one

the social critic that can't keep his mouth shut

criticizes and complains about everything, the living arrangements, the food, the breakdown of the democratic process, corrects the other baboons' use of grammar, talks a lot of bullshit. *But:* The crafty baboon doesn't have the will, skill, courage, or prestige to *do* anything about it, he can only talk up a storm, raise hell until one of the alphas gets sick of his yabber and knocks 'em one upside the head. . . .

But let me tell you, for all his lack of will and skill, the little fucker's got a sex drive like you wouldn't believe, which of course is a problem 'cause all the good women are already spoken for by one of the *alpha* in the tribe, but the little fucker's got to get off somehow *so:*

What he *does* —

And *this.*

is.

fascinating —

What he *does* —

is he *waits*. . . .

At the crack of dawn

while the baboon kids are still asleep
and while the females are packin' up lunchboxes for the alphas' hunt
The Crafty Baboon sleeps with one eye open
watching the whole thing,
waiting . . .
He watches the "good-bye-have-a-nice-day-at-work" kisses,
he watches the alphas march off one by one into the jungle
he watches the females on the porch, wearing their aprons
and waving their good-byes
you'd think it was the fuckin' Brady Bunch . . .
And the horny little fucker lies in wait like that
'til he sees the last purple-assed alpha
disappear through the trees.
Which is his *cue.*
His eyes pop wide open,
he springs up on his hind legs
and the little fucker's up and at 'em.
Heart beating like he's on crack
Can't tell if he's grinning or grimacing
but either way he's so worked up
it looks like his face is about to shatter into a thousand shards.
And he starts chanting to himself
I'M THE MILKMAN
I'M THE PLUMBER
I'M THE PIZZA BOY
I'M THE UPS GUY
I'M THE CABLE GUY
and one by one he starts fucking everything in sight
all those unattainable, spoken-for alpha females
Yeah, he fucks everything in sight *but*
he can't *enjoy* it 'cause . . .
the *alphas* might come home
unannounced any second
and if one of the alphas *caught* him . . .
whhheyyll. . . .

So while he's bouncing up and down like a lunatic pogo stick, he keeps looking over his shoulder
can't concentrate
can't savor the moment . . .

doesn't notice the "are-you-done-yet" look on the chick's face
the tiniest rustling of leaves sets off a paranoia in him
that'd make J. Edgar Hoover envious. . . .
That's how he spends his whole day, day after day:
Paranoid, sweating, a tangle of nerves
heartbeat away from having a coronary,
fucking everything in sight . . .
But incapable of taking an ounce of pleasure in it. . . .
Ohhh . . .
The footage in the documentary was un. b. *liev*able.
And
you don't even want to *know*
what happens when the Crafty Baboon gets caught in the act.
I never knew flesh and fur could be torn up like paper.

IN THE SAWTOOTHS

Dano Madden

More information on this playwright may be found in the "Meet Our Authors" tab at www.smithandkraus.com.

Dramatic
Darin Williams, thirty

Darin is an all-American guy whose life has fallen apart as a result of his four-year-old daughter's accidental death. His wife, Val, won't see him, and their marriage is teetering on the brink of divorce. Darin has been staying with his loyal and obsessive-compulsive friend, Oby. Following a fight with Oby, Darin disappears recklessly into the night. After searching into the wee hours of the morning, Oby finally finds Darin in the middle of a Boise public park. Here, Darin confesses to Oby where he went.

DARIN: I went to our house. Looking for Val. Why the fuck would she be there? All those pictures on the wall . . . I puked everywhere. So I drove to her parents' house. I know she's there. I know she has to be there. Walking up those fucking front steps where I used to leave flowers for her in high school. All I was thinking was, please, God, let me see my wife. Let me see my wife let me see my wife let me see my wife. I rang the bell and I knocked and knocked and knocked please let me see my wife — And the door opened.

My mother-in-law. And I said please can I see my please can I see my wife and she started to close the door and I stopped it with my foot and please can I see my wife please just let me see my wife — And she said, "That girl should still be here. You should've been watching her. Val doesn't want to see you." And she slammed the door in my face.

Goddamn it Oby! No one ever drives down our street. No one ever drives down it. It happened so fast. Never. How could I have — Oby . . . Val told me to put her to bed, she thought I was putting her to bed. But you can't waste summer nights. You can't. We always played hide and seek. You aren't supposed to go to bed early on summer nights —

I just, Sonya wanted to — No one ever drives down our street, no one ever drives down our street no one ever drives down our street — No one ever no one ever no one ever no one ever —

IN THE SAWTOOTHS
Dano Madden

Dramatic
Oby Patterson, thirty

Oby is an insecure, obsessive-compulsive guy. His friend Darin's four-year-old daughter was recently killed in an accident. Darin's wife won't see him, and he is staying with Oby. Darin is lying crumpled underneath a blanket on Oby's living-room floor. Oby has no idea what to say to Darin, who is in a grief-stricken state. Here, he tries.

OBY: I never played T-ball. Most kids start with T-ball. My brother started with T-ball and he was a star. I started with baseball. I liked my glove and I liked being outside, but I knew nothing about the rules. I was terrified at every practice. Our coach really really wanted us to win. He wasn't so patient with kids who didn't understand. He yelled at me a lot. Coach would put me in all these different positions. He never realized that he just needed to explain one position to me. So, at one practice, he wanted me to play catcher. We were doing some base running drill, and I think the catcher was supposed to guard against people trying to steal. I know this now. But then . . . I had no fucking clue. So I put on all the gear. And I went to home plate and Coach was pitching and there were all of these base runners and I was so scared. He probably gave me some instruction, which I probably didn't understand. And then he started pitching to me. All I could remember, from watching the other kid who played catcher, was that he would occasionally jump up, rip his mask off, and look around. So. When coach pitched to me I caught it, jumped up, and ripped my mask off. I looked around with the ball cocked in my hand. And Coach was so happy. "Good! Good, Oby!" So I kept doing the same thing. On every pitch. Jump up. Throw the mask into the dirt. Look around. I don't think I ever actually threw the ball. Coach moved me to right field after the drill. Catch it. Jump up. Throw the mask. Look alive. That's how you play catcher.

LOST GENERATION
Don Nigro

Dramatic
Ernest, late twenties

In Paris, in the late 1920s, Ernest Hemingway is in the middle of an ongoing and increasingly bitter confrontation with his friend Scott Fitzgerald's beautiful and talented but slightly mad wife, Zelda. Zelda has been making fun of what she sees as his absurdly over-the-top attempts to glorify his own masculine image, accusing him of exaggerating his war experiences in his writing and of being a compulsive liar and a ruthless, treacherous, and dishonest self-promoter. There is also a good deal of unspoken sexual tension between them that is just about to burst out. This is an angry Hemingway defending himself and his work to her.

ERNEST: In Milan I saw a blown-up munitions factory. There was a barbed wire fence with meat hanging on it. Arms, legs, backs, heads. Guts strung all over. One girl, completely naked, not a scratch on her, just the head was gone. I saw that and I wrote about it. And what does Scott write about? Parties. Jesus Christ. Is that what a writer is supposed to be for? That's the truth? You want to know the truth? Here's the truth. Everything good that ever happened to me I made up. But all the bad stuff is true. It's easy to write the truth. You've just got to be a great liar. The minute you put pen to paper, it's a lie before the ink dries. It's got to be a lie because it can't be what happened — it's ink on paper. Every story is a lie. But some lies are better than others. Some of the lies we write are better than what really happened because they give us access to parts of ourselves that are truer than we could possibly have understood if somebody didn't lie to us that way. It's all betrayal. All writing is betrayal. Betrayal is truth. My writing is a magnificent betrayal. Therefore, my writing is truth. And anybody who gets in the way needs to be killed. Anything else you want to know about the truth?

MAHIDA'S EXTRA KEY TO HEAVEN

Russell Davis

More information on this playwright may be found in the "Meet Our Authors" tab at www.smithandkraus.com.

Dramatic
Ramin, late twenties to early thirties

Ramin, a young Iranian, has come to Edna's house in a small coastal village to find his sister, Mahida, and bring her home. He learns that she is out for a walk with Edna's son, Thomas, whom he does not know. While he waits for Mahida's return, he and Edna find that they have little in common, and the discomfort and wariness between them grows.

RAMIN: God is in all this your money buys? There's God in your television programs? Your Hollywood? Your advertisements on your buses or magazines? These photographs and posters with young men and women, even boys and girls, touching each other while they wear only underpants? This is God to you? To advertise like this? Everywhere I walk in your country, everywhere I look, I see something to make people think of sex, or to take a drug. To suggest these things. This is what you want your children to see? How they should grow up? With all this false allurement? . . .

This enticement? You might as well hand your children now a new alphabet coloring book. The letter "A" could be a picture of adultery or anal sex. How to do these things. The letter "B" could be bellyache or backache. "C" would be copulation or cancer. This would at least be truthful. How can you teach a child to be deaf and blind to what is all around? What surrounds them in your country? What must surely infect how they think, what they choose. And what you now want to surround all the rest of the world with. . . .

Oh, yes. You think what you do stops here on these shores? This is your freedom? Your sprawl? To spread out across the whole world? To change what we see in our own lands, what is in our own thoughts, or the thoughts of our children and women?

Hah.

This is your supply-side economics? Your foreign investment laws?

This is more than an invasion, I think. Some soldiers who come by for a century or so. No, this is an attempt to remake the world. To change forever the very face of the earth. The ground we stand on. To manipulate all the minds of men and to brush aside all opposing culture. To make us all in your image. What your land here has become.

MEATBALL HERO

Richard Vetere

More information on this playwright may be found in the "Meet Our Authors" tab at www.smithandkraus.com.

Comic
Raymond, midthirties

Raymond is a rough-around-the-edges, self-made New York City businessman. He wears a suit but is more street-wise than white collar. Here, he asks the French waiter to bring him something substantial to eat instead of the "sissy" French food he has been served. Also, he realizes that he has lost his date, Holly, to the obvious charms of the French waiter, but Raymond doesn't care. Like the legendary American cowboy, he prefers to follow his American roots, meaning he'd rather enjoy the substantial pleasures of "man food" — a meatball hero, alone — than impress Holly by eating "sissy food."

RAYMOND: A meatball hero is an essential to everything! It is round, like the earth. Like the sun and moon. Like the wheel, like a baseball, like your head, like your eyes, like your balls, like a great pair of tits! Juicy, tender, round, got it? Like Buddha's belly and Saturn's rings. And in a meatball is meat. Real meat. Beef, pork, or veal. And you know what? You put things in the meat. Good, tasty things. Like ricotta and mozzarella cheese and pignola nuts. You don't want a spongy meatball. You want to drown it in flavor with a good meat sauce and a hero roll from an Italian bakery. And you don't want your meatball made by a machine. No, it has to be handmade. And it can't be weighed down with bread crumbs and leaden with the wrong cheese. It's food a man can sink his teeth into. It's masculine, virile. That's what a man needs to eat to fill his belly, not this sissy food! And more than that, a meatball is a hero. Yes, a hero, Jack. Do you people have any idea what a hero is? `

MISTAKES WERE MADE
Craig Wright

Comic
Felix Artifex, forties to sixties

Felix is a wheeling-dealing Broadway producer. He specializes in revivals of the classics featuring movie or television stars (such as Suzanna Somers in Medea *and Tony Danza in* The Master Builder*). He is on the phone with the playwright of a new play he is producing about the French Revolution and is explaining his "philosophy" of producing.*

FELIX: Steven, here's the deal: life is unbearable and short. Yes, life is unbearable and short and people wanna be entertained. Meanwhile, you're in the Heartland, with your wife and kid, working your day job but getting ideas, which is what I love about you. You've got your cute little family, your ten thousand things, your grocery lists, strollers, your torn-up floors, but you're sitting there thinking, "Maybe the French Revolution would be fun to put onstage, I'll call it *Mistakes Were Made*, there'll be a cast of fifty with a guillotine, a star drop, and a horse, it'll be about freedom and responsibility, Thermidor and Fructidor, impossible to produce unless handled very carefully, GREAT." Meanwhile, movie stars, Steven, the snot-nosed, silk-diapered, emerald-green gods of our time, are sitting by pools in Beverly Hills thinking, "I have everything I've ever wanted, I have the love and adoration of billions, but I don't know why I'm ALIVE!" And me, Steven, little me, I'm sitting here in New York City, the hub of the Western World, with the razor-sharp bottom of this whole pyramid resting on my eyeball, you know, I've got all these myriad vectors, Steven, bearing down on my little watery eyeball, I'm sitting here seeing all these forces at work, and all I'm doing, kid, all I'm doing all day long, is trying like hell with my two free hands to do whatever I can to draw all these disparate, tragic, lonely, lovely forces together because for me, Steven, poor sucker that I am, this is my curse, there's no greater pleasure in life I can imagine than to make this play happen onstage!

MISTAKES WERE MADE
Craig Wright

Comic
Felix Artifex, forties to sixties

Felix is a wheeling-dealing Broadway producer. He specializes in revivals of the classics featuring movie or television stars (such as Suzanna Somers in Medea *and Tony Danza in* The Master Builder*). He is on the phone with the playwright of a new play he is producing about the French Revolution and is explaining why he has to rewrite his play to suit the demands of the television star he has engaged to play the lead.*

FELIX: Steven, what I think will make Johnny happy — and I may embroider a little bit as I go — is maybe you start with this kid at the beginning, right, this new character of *yours*, in a new scene *you'll* make great where he maybe says good-bye to, uh — his little, uh, sister, you know, as she's dying? I just throw that out there. You know, maybe they're at a, uh, festival, you know, in the park, and guys are making speeches, you know, like, uh, "This isn't fair! That's not right! Down with the King," you know, "Oui, oui, oui!" And as he's listening, you know, kind of suspicious of all these jokers, she wanders off with her little blue balloon, and she falls and hits her head by a fountain, right? It's an idea. And, uh, lying there on the ground with the blood pooling behind her little, cracked, wet, dripping head, she's, like, you know, "Make sure the revolution happens, Philippe" or something like that — you'll figure it out; far be it from me to write dialogue; you're the artist; what's important, though is, Steven, *she* had hope, right, and she died but now *he's* fucked up and stuck living, and we just set him on a course like that, right? From that moment there by the fountain, he's haunted and his course is *set*, and then we just stick with him, you know, at the edges of the first few scenes as we go along, keeping everything else pretty much the same except now *he's* there, right, this brand-new being *you* have built into the system, this haunted French *homo sapiens*, taking it all in as things are getting revved up with the revolution, you know, like, "Ooh, wow, what's that? Where are those guys running with that cannon? *Zut alors,*" you know? Maybe he's got a baguette or something he's always noshing on, that's a funny detail, take it or leave it — anyway, the thing is, Steven, is his poor dead daughter is always on his mind, Steven, *always* on his mind, and maybe you even play that echo in his — I'm sorry, sister — right, his sister — that's what I meant, but maybe you play that echo in his head, you know? "Make sure the revolution happens, Philippe. Make sure the revolution happens." — you know what I'm saying? It's just an idea. And what happens is, in this model, is he gradually goes from being this street kid who's, you know, just, Pierre's buddy, you know, being carried along by events —

Robespierre's buddy — whatever — carried along by events, to be, being, you know, by the time you get to the Tennis Court scene maybe, the starring role. Yeah. Maybe he's the one who renames the months of the year, ya know? That could be a fun twist. Maybe it's a song? That could be extremely cute, you know?

(Sung:) Thermidor, Fructidor, where'd we ever get these names? No, I am not mentally ill, Steven; I am imaginative, hopeful, and driven.

NEW JERUSALEM

David Ives

Dramatic
Baruch Spinoza, twenty-four

Spinoza, on trial for spreading ideas heretical to both Jew and Christian, here confides to a friend the details of his spiritual awakening.

SPINOZA: I didn't stop. Life stopped *me*. You see, when my father died, it suddenly seemed to me as if all the things I wanted in the world were utterly meaningless. Empty. Futile. I couldn't see the point of stepping out the door each day, much less becoming a rabbi. Then the business got into trouble. A cargo of dates fell to the English. Pirates took another ship. I couldn't pay my father's debts. I began to think that God had abandoned me. Then one day sitting in the garden at the Spinning Wheel, I saw that all these concerns of mine were actually neither good nor bad. My problem wasn't death or pirates or falling prices. The problem was letting myself be affected by these things. So I decided to find out whether there was anything that was *actually* good. Ultimately good. A good that would erase the distinction between good and bad. Something that, once I found it, would provide continuous, supreme, and everlasting happiness. It seemed to me upon reflection that there are three things men tend to pursue in this life: riches, honor, and pleasure. Riches are more precarious than being a Jew in Amsterdam. A shipload of sugar sinks off of Brazil and you're ruined. Honor depends on the opinions of other men. There are men in this world who'd honor you for cutting other men's throats in a marketplace. Why should I be a slave to those men's values? Sensual pleasure isn't continuous and everlasting happiness. It's an endless search for more pleasure, or greater pleasure. So I was left with nothing except my father's debts. I realized that God hadn't abandoned me. I realized that I had abandoned God. I realized that true happiness can only come from the mind's attempt to comprehend God. I realized that life is only meaningful insofar as it is part of God.

NEXT FALL
Geoffrey Nauffts

Dramatic
Adam, forty-five

Adam's boyfriend Luke is in a coma due to a car accident. Luke, much younger than Adam, is a born-again Christian, which has caused friction between the two men, as Adam is a determined atheist. Here, Adam is talking to Brandon, a friend of Luke's who does not accept his relationship with Adam.

ADAM: Actually, there is something else . . . Do you have a second? God, this is awkward . . . Is it OK if I just sort of dive in here? OK . . . So, Luke and I have been together a little over four years now — who would have thunk it, right? And things are great, all things considered. More than great, really, I mean, we've got our issues, but who doesn't? I mean, he's still not out to his parents, which is just boring at this point, but frankly, they don't seem like the kind of folks I really want to spend a holiday with, so . . . Plus, he's out everywhere else in life, so it's mostly normal. It's a negotiation, like any relationship. He lets me watch CNN 24/7, I let him watch that show where people hop across the big, rubber b alls and fall into the mud. He puts up with my tirades about the health care reform, I put up with his Martha Stewart magazines. He drops a fan on my face in the middle of the night. . . . We make compromises, that's all I'm saying. He's not even that extreme as far as all the Jesus stuff goes. He's pro-choice, he believes in stem cell research. I think he may even vote for a Democrat in the next election. Oh, and we're talking about having a baby now, too. Well, I'm talking, but he's nodding his head a lot. So, it's mostly good. It's just the praying after sex. *(A beat.)* That's the one little quirk I'm still having a hard time with. *(Another beat.)* I know we've never talked about this kind of thing before, you and I. I mean, I don't even know if you're openly gay . . . Or unopenly gay, even. I assume you're gay . . . Or gayish. Gay friendly, at least. So, if you are . . . and you do . . . I mean, is that something you do, too? Pray after sex? *(A beat.)* You don't have to answer. I'm sorry. It's just something that's really been bugging me lately. I mean, it's not like I see it or anything. It's not like he's kneeling at the side of the bed flogging himself with a leather switch. I wish, right? No, it's more like he feels dirty and silently asks for forgiveness. *(A beat.)* And it's not like it's all the time either. In fact, he hardly ever does it. But still, even once in a while, it's weird, you know? Because of the whole . . . It's like, *really*? That's what you have to do? I mean, all the other stuff I can sort of deal with. But the praying after sex? It just sort of makes everything feel a little tainted somehow. I mean, how am I ever gonna feel loved for real with, you know, all that in the way? *(Another beat.)* OK, I'll stop . . . You talk . . . If you want to. I know I'm sort of dumping this all out there, so . . . But, please. If you have any . . . pearls . . . I'd be glad for anything.

9 CIRCLES
Bill Cain

Dramatic
Reeves, early twenties

Reeves is a young soldier in Iraq speaking with a woman army psychiatrist. He has a problem: He wants to kill everyone. The psychiatrist has a problem treating him. If he tells her his problem, she has to send him back to the States, and he desperately wants to stay with his unit in Iraq. He is demanding her sympathy for a problem he cannot name.

REEVES: If I had a bullet in my head and I were lying here, you'd feel bad for me.

(Silence.)

If I were laying here on your floor bleeding from the head, *how long* would you feel bad for me?

(No response.)

Because — out there — they put a bullet in me — they'd celebrate for a month. A year. Fuck. Forever. They kill me, they get to go to God, directly to God, do not stop at any checkpoints. When those construction workers got killed — they hung their body parts from the bridge and they danced their asses off for days. Now you want to talk about sympathy — I've got all kinds of sympathy for that because that is *exactly* how I feel about them. We want each other dead. Now you — you've got all the sympathy in the world for a dying sergeant — fuck — ANY BODY CAN FEEL SYMPATHY FOR THE GOOD GUY. He doesn't *need* your sympathy. He's got a wife and a kid for that. But that guy who shot him — I want to fucking kill him over and over. That's what goes on in my head and you've got no sympathy for that. "Don't tell me that. You're on your own with that," and you know what that means? You've got no sympathy for the one thing that *needs* it here and I don't want to make him an excuse.

I think I've *always* wanted to kill everybody. Him dying just makes me think I'm finally going to do it.

THE OPTIMIST

Jason Chimonides

More information on this playwright may be found in the "Meet Our Authors" tab at www.smithandkraus.com.

Seriocomic
Declan, twenty-five

Declan, a pedantic and puerile graduate student, holds forth on the dangers of idealism. Here, he is ranting to his twin brother, Noel, that he doesn't care about anything except getting laid.

DECLAN: Answer me this first . . . I *entreat* ye! OK, sure, I can anatomize the philosophy of Schopenhauer, I can spew nineteenth-century critical bullhockey, I can enunciate arcanna with the *best* of 'em, but who gives a shit ultimately, because all I really wanna do is get *laid*! *(Beat.)* I see a juicy ass and I just wanna poke a straw in it and slurp away. Why am I like that? Why am I such a brute, huh?! Why are we all? *(A beat.)* . . .

I've had an epiphany! It happened today on Hambone's boat. We were frolicking in the brine, Noel, I was really quite a lot of fun, you missed out . . . anyway . . . see, see, what became clear to me today as I thought on't . . . no, not *just* clear, but rather *limpid* and *crystalline,* is that the worst atrocities ever perpetrated upon humankind, you name it, the great evils, right? . . . genocide, subjugation, whatever . . . circumcision, these have all *categorically* been hatched, not by devils . . . but by *dreamers (Slight beat.) Beware of them,* I say! *Be-ware* of *anyone* who tells you that they *"believe"* in anything or worse, who makes ringing declarations attributed to the first person plural! "We"? "Our"? *"Us"*? *DAN-ger. (Slight beat.)* Because whether they're an assistant manager at Taco Bell or leader of the free world, they have the ability to inflict *unyielding* pain to everyone around them. Look at history: Look at the monsters, the butchers, the anti-Christs, these people had something very simple in common . . . they were a lot like the Little Mermaid. *(Slight beat.)* Or Peter Pan. Or *Quasimodo.* They all had *dreams* . . . weird-ass, untenable, ABSURD DREAMS! *(Slight beat.)* The "Aryan race"?! "From each according to his abilities, to each according to his *needs*"?! *Democracy!* C'mon! The world doesn't work like that!

OUR HOUSE
Theresa Rebeck

Seriocomic
Wes, thirties to forties

Wes is the high-powered head of programming for a major television network. Here, he tells his board of directors that if he had his way, the network wouldn't be broadcasting any news at all, which they are required to do under the terms of their FCC license.

WES: The fact is — I am told — the reality is — that we are required by the FCC to broadcast a certain number of hours of news, to the public, in exchange for the right to use the airwaves. Now. Clearly, I didn't make the rule up!

No one checked in with me, when they invented America. And do I object to this rule, this so-called law of the land? I do. Why? Because staying informed, in America, is optional. No one forces anyone to read the newspaper! And they are consequently, blessedly, being permitted to fold, to go the way of the buggy whip and the penny whistle. It's not required to watch the evening news! Americans are free. Airwaves are free. How do those two fundamental truths add up to a requirement to broadcast the news? I ask, and ask, and ask. And no one answers.

(A beat.) There is a fundamental mistake here. Television, in its inception, seemed to present itself as a tool for humanity's further development, offering profound opportunities for communication, education, entertainment. But as time passed, and we became aware of its true nature, the tragic misunderstandings which surrounded these assumptions revealed themselves. Television is not our subject; it is not our creation! We are not looking at it! It is looking at us! And if we are real — I mean, if we are real — then television is what makes us real. Because it's hyper-real. And hyper-reality is not free. It's really expensive to run a network! And you know what is NOT an option, in America? Profitability. When the FCC and its misunderstandings and misconceptions about what television is get in the way of our profits, I say: we stand up. And demand our rights. So. We're cutting seven hundred jobs out of the news division. There will still be news! But it will be news on our terms. Airwaves are free. Americans are free. The news is not free.

OUR HOUSE
Theresa Rebeck

Dramatic
Merv, twenties to thirties

Merv lives in a communal house with three other people. He has become obsessed with television and has gone crazy, shooting and killing one housemate and holding the others hostage. He demands to meet Jennifer, the local news network anchorwoman, whom he idolizes. Here, he is ranting to her about why he has done what he has done.

MERV: How it came about? I don't know. She wanted to turn off my TV.

Do you think that television makes people stupid, Jennifer? Alice here keeps insisting that it does and she is sincerely annoying, but I'm starting to think she has a point. Because I think watching television — and I watch a lot, I sit around and watch it like all the time, and I'm not like a brainiac or anything but I am not a stupid person but I'll tell you, Jennifer — you think about things like Moby Dick, that used to be like, popular entertainment — not popular, I think Moby Dick was actually a flop but that's you know, normal people, you and me, used to hang out reading interesting books and having conversation, just hanging out with someone like Benjamin Franklin and shooting the shit, that's what they did to relax. . . .

My parents were really nice people this isn't their fault, although I had this older sister, don't get me started. But that's not, psychology isn't news, Jennifer! Or maybe it is. I don't know anymore. I think that frankly, television doesn't just make us stupid, it also makes us depressed. All those bright colors! And everyone looks so pretty and and real. Real, how does television do that, make people look hyper-real. It makes you just want to climb in there. But then the shows are all so depressing and moronic, you end up — if that is reality? Why not just blow our brains out . . .

And once that thought occurs to you, that you could kill yourself, theoretically, you could kill other people, there's a lot of killing going on out there, you could get in on it, and then you go into a gun store, you can buy guns at Walmarts, if you really want to know, Jennifer, they don't cost anything! . . .

They cost less than a PlayStation 3! They cost less than . . . killing people, killing yourself, killing a whole bunch of people, costs nothing at all in America. Why don't you put that on television? As long as all you care about is money, why don't you talk about how cheap it is to kill people? . . .

But you don't, you don't put anything, and I understand, it's a drag, to talk about death, on the other hand here you are and it's not because you love St. Louis — it's because death sells. Those guys in Mumbai, that's how you pronounce it, they didn't care about getting the word out about Kashmir! They just wanted to be on television. Because that's the equation. Violence equals TV Time. You don't even have to have a reason anymore!

PARASITE DRAG

Mark Roberts

More information on this playwright may be found in the "Meet Our Authors" tab at www.smithandkraus.com.

Dramatic
Ronnie, twenties

Parasite Drag *is about a midwestern family that has come together because one of the adult children is dying of AIDS. Ronnie talks about the last time he saw her.*

ROBBIE: I haven't seen her since she got out of that rehab in Chicago, I think was the last time. She got out on a Monday and was back on that shit by Wednesday night. She had hooked up with some dirtbag on the south side. I drove into the projects to pick her up. Man, she was a mess. Filthy dirty. Arms all bruised up. I wanted to get out of there, so I told her to grab her stuff. She picked up a greasy paper bag. It had a shirt and a couple of odds and ends. And that was it. That was all she had in the world. Took her out to eat. Watched her smoke about a hundred and twenty Salems and then drove her back to rehab. I remember when I dropped her off I told her to take care of herself. And she looked at me for the longest time. With this puzzled look on her face. Like she had no idea what I was talking about.

Drying up and blowing away.

PARASITE DRAG
Mark Roberts

Dramatic
Ronnie, twenties

> Parasite Drag *is about a midwestern family that has come together because one of the adult children is dying of AIDS. Ronnie is the reprobate. Gene is studying for the ministry. Here, Ronnie talks about Gene.*

RONNIE: I wish you would have known Gene as a kid. He was a whole different person. Little entertainer he was. Used to always walk around wearing a hat, or a big coat, or some getup. He'd memorize whole routines from *The Jackie Gleason Show* or some shit, and then he'd act 'em out whenever we had company. And he was good, too. He'd do all the voices. Real comical. Little ham. There's home movies of it somewhere. He was a funny kid. Then after our mom died, he changed. I mean, we all changed, but Gene was the most drastic. He became an old man. I remember we had this dog, Lightning. German shepherd. He used to chase every car that drove past the house. Get right up on it. Right next to the tires, at full speed. Dumb fucking dog. Well, one day a Charles Chips truck drives past the house . . . Did you ever have those? Potato chips, came in big metal containers? I loved them things. Barbecue. Anyway, old Lightning gets sucked under the tires of that thing and it squashes the shit out of him. Middle of the street. Eyes hanging out. Guts coming out its ass. Brutal. Gene comes running over, crying. He was . . . I don't know, thirteen, maybe. Bawling his eyes out, and screaming to God to save this dog. Laying his hands on him trying to heal him. And that poor animal was gone. He was gasping out a few bloody breaths, but it was over for Lightning. And I tried to scoop him up and carry him to the yard, but Gene wouldn't let me near him. Kept screaming that God was gonna save him. God was gonna heal him. And the dog was suffering. Driving him to the vet would have been futile. So, I grabbed the snow shovel out of the garage, kicked Gene away from him and put him out of his misery.

PRAYER FOR MY ENEMY

Craig Lucas

More information on this playwright may be found in the "Meet Our Authors" tab at www.smithandkraus.com.

Dramatic
Billy, twenties

Billy is a young man who has gone to serve in Iraq to escape his abusive father. Here, he finally stands up to the old man.

BILLY: For my whole life I tried to do nothing. Like you just said. Stay still. Be invisible. Do less harm. The invisible man you gave me with all the organs — that was me. That why you gave it to me? You know what they called us at school, me and Marianne? The No Ones. I had no skin. I had no anything. Just all the bad that God could see inside. I'm like that now, like you, I can see into everything. Mom said you couldn't, but you could. When Taddy and I were fooling around, you knew it. That's when you started calling me all those names. And now . . . I can see through everyone; I can see through your shit too. Civility. I'm the civil one. I'm the contemplative one. When was I less than civil? Who are you talking to? It can't be me. The only person you ever were interested in talking to is you. Charity? To aid the needy and suffering? *Sacrifice*? I'm at war! I'm offering my life. For you! I was always offering it with you around. What good is charity and cleaning up rooms when a whole species wants to kill itself? We're both bad, you and me, we're both killers now. I always wanted you to give me a legacy. That's your legacy: murder. Soul death. Give life to some little babies — little boy, little girl — so you can take your time killing it then tell yourself all is forgiven as you turn your back on the carnage. Take one more look and take that with you into the next life, that'll be my gift to you. *Dad.*

PUSSY BOY

Christine Evans

More information on this playwright may be found in the "Meet Our Authors" tab at www.smithandkraus.com.

Dramatic
Bill, forty

Bill is a working-class single father whose son, Algy, has run away after a beating. He's a carpenter of sorts; here he imagines impressing the local police, who have just evicted his dog-hoarding tenant. But his mind returns to the loss of his wife, who left him before Algy did.

BILL: I would have thrown her out weeks ago, Officer.
If it wasn't for my better nature.
Goes against the grain.
Woman out on the streets.
Smelling like that.
Hard to talk to a woman who smells like a fish.

You must see it all the time. Sir.
Have to fumigate the place now.
Stink of dogs. Bad smells.

Women shouldn't smell.
There's — what have you —
there's a whole industry there —
Just to make them smell good.

Mmmm. Yeah.
Eau de Femme. Mmmm.
Not bad. Not bad.
Funny how it sticks.
Long after the body's gone.
Just as well.
Just the smell.
You smell so good.

(Beat.)
Where are you, honey? Is he good to you?
— Nights like this, I can almost see you.
Almost feel you.
Hard to see in the dark.

Can't see your face any more.
Except when I look at the kid.
That's messed up, don't you think?
Those long, long eyelashes
Wasted on a boy.
But what can I do
When you're so damn gone.

I can still taste you.
You only open up in the dark.
My moonflower, sweet and white.
Them long long legs sliding up my shoulders.
Mmmm.
Close my eyes in the dark and . . .
Oh yes. *(Beat.)*
You sweet-faced lying bitch.

Shoulda kept my eyes open with you.
Look to see what you was looking at over my shoulder.
(Beat.)
Boy's got your eyes.
Your skin
Sometimes I swear he's got your smell.

The smell of lies.
Done all I can to train it outta him.
He's a good boy but he needs a lot of work.
A lot of fucken work to turn out right.
Not like his mama, sneaking off in the dark.

And don't —
Fucking
Come
Back.

PUSSY BOY
Christine Evans

Dramatic
Algy, eleven

Algy is a dreamy young boy who has run away from his violent father, Bill. He has taken shelter with the Dog Lady, who hoards dogs and takes Algy in as a pet. Here, Algy justifies his dad's actions to the Dog Lady, who only intermittently listens. What begins as a straightforward explanation moves toward Algy's own need to untangle for himself the complex knot of love and abuse that ties him to his father — and to work out what to do next.

ALGY: He just wants me to be strong like him. It's training. It's for my own good. He doesn't want me to get soft. *(Beat.)* It's not so bad. I can sleep on my stomach after. I count to a hundred when he does it, it stops hurting after about thirty. *That's* a good trick I learned. It's best not to hold your breath. You can breathe out when the belt comes down, and if you breathe really fast you can sometimes get dizzy and faint, and he stops then. Once I fainted when I was up to forty, he was really worried about me. Are you all right Son, he said and he put his arms all round me, Jesus Son, wake up, come on Son, I'm just trying to help you, please please Jesus. . . . I held my breath and everything was perfect, so perfect like on a seesaw and you balance exactly, your feet are off the ground and you feel like you never ever have to come down. But it always tips and you get heavy again. And you wish and wish you could stay in the air with the sky under your legs and everything . . . but the more you wish the heavier you get — I think if I was a unicorn I could balance there forever.

I wouldn't *wish* 'cause that makes you heavy.
I would be white as amnesia
and when people saw me I would just look at them,
not angry or happy but just . . . looking . . .
And they would slow down —
like they were walking through water —

— And they'd feel all sweet inside and when they blinked I'd disappear.

That's what unicorns do. They disappear.

And they wouldn't remember me but they would keep that sweet feeling inside them. *(Beat.)* He put his arms around me you know. I can still feel his arms all round me like water. He's really strong. I can't feel him belting me, only breathing and counting but I can feel his arms round me. Is that amnesia? But I did have to breathe in the end, and so he knew I was awake, just pretending — and then he was so angry, more angry than before.

(Beat. Quietly.) He's really angry now.

RAVISHED
Don Nigro

Dramatic
Coll, twenties

In this modern retelling of the tale Shakespeare told in "The Rape of Lucrece," Coll, a young man, works for a privately contracted company in a war in a far-off place and has been seriously scarred emotionally by his experiences there. Here, he sits before a fire in the night in that war zone and talks to his fellow worker John Tarquin about his girl back home, Lucrece.

COLL: I close my eyes and try to picture her. I have the photograph, but it's not like her. I mean, it is, but it isn't. It's just one piece of her. One expression on her face, but her face is always different. Her eyes change color in the light. Do you know how when you're with someone you love, it's hard to focus on them? It's like they always somehow get away from you before you can really touch them. Even when you're touching them sometimes you can't really see them because you're so close. You can only see part of them. You can only touch part of them. And then they're gone, and you try to remember, but you can't quite. Not enough. Not clearly enough. They're just these half-remembered fragments in your head, and you can't be satisfied until you see them again. But then perhaps you don't. At some point, you don't. Any time could be the last time. Maybe you know it is, and maybe you don't. I don't want to forget anything. I want to remember all of her, every inch of her flesh. I want to remember how it felt to kiss every part of her. Her lips were soft and full. Her breasts. The moment when she'd uncover her breasts. It was always this miraculous thing. Kissing her. Kissing her stomach. Kissing her back. The way her back tapers down to her waist. Her arms. She has the most beautiful arms. The down on her arms. Her hands. The way she sculpts the air with her hands when she's excited, when she's talking, her hands seem to take on a life of their own. It's like poetry. The way her hands move. I don't want to forget. If I say the words, I won't forget.

She would make this little noise. When I entered her. This very strange little murmur of something like surprise. Fear. Pleasure. Pain. I don't know what exactly it was, but it was an astonishingly erotic thing. And then she'd cry. While we were making love. She'd sob like a child. I don't know why she cried. She wouldn't tell me. I suppose she didn't know. Or maybe she knew, and didn't think it was any of my business. She was a stranger to me, really. The more we made love, the stranger she got. At first I'd be concerned, but then something in me would just take over, and it didn't matter, and she was everything and then she'd kind of disappear. And then when it was over, she'd hold onto me, but she wouldn't look at me. But then finally she would look at me, into my eyes, as if she was trying to remember who I was. As if I was the stranger. It always scared the crap out of me. I just wanted to get away from her. I suppose it was guilt. As if I'd done something terrible to her. As if I'd violated her, somehow. But then the lust would come again. She'd be sitting there naked on the bed, with her arms around her legs, her face resting against her knees, looking so small and helpless and lost, as if somebody had just done something so terrible to her that nothing could ever make it right again. And then I'd feel the lust rising up in me again. And I'd kiss her back and run my hands along her arms and kiss her hair, kiss her neck, and she'd stay curled up tight, not letting me in. Not letting me in. She never let me in.

REENTRY
Emily Ackerman and KJ Sanchez

Dramatic
Tommy, midtwenties

ReEntry *is a documentary play taken entirely from interviews with members of the U.S. Marine Corps and their families. Tommy is a USMC staff sergeant who was injured in an IED explosion that left him blind and with limited use of one of his arms and that also killed one of his colleagues. He has been deployed multiple times and considers himself a career marine. He has an easy wit, a deep commitment to the military, and absolutely no self-pity.*

TOMMY: Around here people don't treat you differently when they find out you're in the Marine Corps. Northern California some lady called me a baby killer. I was like in a bar and some lady asked me what I did, I'm in the Marine Corps. Oh, you kill people. And I'm like, I don't like to talk about that. Oh you're a baby killer. And I kinda got offended at first. And then I was like, I'm not gonna let her ignorance get to me, not gonna let it ruin my day. So she's "you're a baby killer." Yeah, got any kids? AAAAH! She went off. I'm like, look, I'm not a baby killer, OK? I just do what I gotta do.

People will bitch about us, you know, we drink a lot, we party. Work hard party hard. Party like rock stars fucking like porn stars type of thing. Cause you know you are going to be in some shit-hole desert, it's going to be hot, it's going to be boring, it's going to be dangerous, so why not have a good time while we are here, you know?

I deployed five times. Cinco. I came back single two times, and after that I was either engaged or married. The first time I came back, I bought a car. I came back, my buddy picked me up, surprised my parents and then we just went out and drank. I had just turned twenty-one. The second time, you know, you just appreciate life a little bit more but you're still kinda edgy. A lot of guys who go into big cities get flustered, don't want to be around big crowds. They'd go to bars, but small bars like this, not big "excuse me excuse me" kinda bars. They'd stay away from that as much as possible. Because you can't control that environment. When I was out there, I had full control of everything like a ringmaster — I'd radio in, "Hey we got these guys here, these guys there." And you come back and you're like, "This guy keeps looking at me weird." The third time I came back, I was a little conceited, whatever. The fourth time I came back, my wife was pregnant. I just laid in bed with her and rubbed her tummy all night. I rubbed her tummy and tried to catch up to what I missed. That time I was more mellow, 'cause my son was being born, so I was just focused on that. This time coming back sucked.

REENTRY

Emily Ackerman and KJ Sanchez

Dramatic
John, early thirties

> *ReEntry* is a documentary play taken entirely from interviews with members of the U.S. Marine Corps and their families. John is a USMC captain. He is a career marine and an officer. He has returned home from a particularly hard deployment and is finding it increasingly difficult to be around civilians. John is a very intelligent, intense personality with a real sense of righteousness and a sharp sense of humor. He does not suffer fools.

JOHN: Oh, man, when I first got home? The skateboarders? Those stupid little faggy skater shitheads wearing girl's pants? Not that fags are bad . . . it's just the way I talk. But have you seen these kids with these fucking pants? They were probably maybe thirteen or fourteen. They were skateboarding in a brand-new development that was just built, and they were basically trying to grind on the curb, which was a freshly painted, like, brand-new, like, thing. And I ask them, I go, "What are you doin'?" They're like, *(In whiny, lispy kid voice.)* "Yeah, well we heard this is a good place to skate." . . .

"You live here?"

"No."

"What the fuck are you doing?"

"We're skatin' dude, we heard it was a good place."

"It's not. So, you don't live here, and you're here fuckin' up my brand-new, freshly painted sidewalk. You pay for that shit?"

"No."

"Get the fuck out."

"Dude! You don't have to like, you don't have to like, swear at us."

"You don't have to do anything but leave, right fuckin' now."

You know, just a punk kid that doesn't do like, anything. . . .

And the kid is like, "Oh yeah dude, like, whatever." And I'm like, "Don't come back. If you COME back, see that cliff over there? I'm gonna launch you. I will stop your heart, son." . . .

It was really like, it was kinda intense. It went from like, zero, to fuckin' homicidal in about three seconds. . . .

What can people actually do to support the troops? Quit bitchin'. I like the, uh, flag waving, that happens for about a month. And then nothing. If I don't get my three dollar Starbucks, and get to work on time, and pay less than whatever for a gallon of gas, then I am going to bitch and moan and cry. Everybody is so fuckin' spoiled. I think the majority of Americans are a bunch of whining pussies. People watch too much fuckin' TV. Like ridiculous amounts. Like, do I even care who is on *Dancing with the Stars*? I didn't even know that was a fucking show. People are like, "OH! On *Dancing with the . . .*" I'm like, "Are you fucking retarded? What did you have for dinner yesterday? A BIG MAC. Go fuck yourself." So when the kid that's grinding my sidewalk is like, dude, that's not cool — It's easier for me to launch him over a cliff and not even worry about it. He's worthless at this point to me. And when you've pulled one of your marines, who just got his legs blown off, out of that shit, and he's only a few years older than that douche with his skateboard that is never going to do anything with his life, it kinda makes you not give a fuck about hurting that retard's "feelings." . . .

Everything you people get so excited about is fucking pointless. Like, fucking recycling. Go anywhere else on earth and there is so much shit burning in the streets — there's so much crap just burning everywhere, you look at like an old car just burning in the streets and the smoke it generates and it's like, YEAH I'm glad I recycled that motherfuckin' milk bottle! You know? It's pointless. If you're so bored with yourself that you get excited about recycling then you need to get a hobby. One person recycling some fuckin' soda cans makes about as much sense as a *Tyrannosaurus rex* trying to take a shit on a napkin so as not to make a mess.

What should we do? You want my honest opinion? Everyone that is pissing us off we should nuke the shit out of them and turn their country into glass and then build it in our own fashion!

Right now, I'm just happy that I'm not being shot at. But at the same time, I'm kinda upset that I don't have anyone to shoot. It's like, yeah, I do wish I had a relationship, a girlfriend. I do. But how do we marry these two extremes? Like back in the day all the women wanted to be with a gladiator, right? Well, try to take a gladiator to goddamned dinner. But for the most part it's like, you are trained to be a certain way, to do certain things, and then you are just supposed to turn that off and go back to society with the rest of you pussies.

THE REST OF THE NIGHT
Robert Lewis Vaughan

Dramatic
Miller, late twenties to early thirties

Not able to settle into the life of a dying town and not able to leave it either, Miller falls into alcoholism and finds false courage in the bottle. Already well on his way to destroying his marriage to Malia and his relationship with his young son, Eric, Miller sinks lower and begins to blame everyone else for his trouble. He decides it's time to teach Eric what he thinks is a valuable life lesson by confining him to the doghouse and nailing the door shut.

MILLER: I want you to listen to me. I want you to listen real hard. You start payin' attention to me. I'm gonna get us outta here one of these days. I will. Just you watch me. We'll have everything I ever promised you we'd have. I'll be a success. We just have to get away from here. They're all keepin' us down, boy. Your mama thinks she's doin' what's right, but she don't know nothin', you hear me? She thinks she's got to take care of us. She thinks I can't take care of us — she's holdin' me back 'cause she don't believe in me neither. . . . Everybody always tells you what to do. Everybody always thinks they know what's best for you and they just gotta tell you. They tell you what to do, then they walk away from you and laugh at you when you turn around and try to do somethin'. I'll tell you what, boy — you just listen to me, and you do what I tell you. I love you, son. . . . I will get us outta here . . . I got me a man who knows about a little place up by Salida, Colorado. He's lookin' for somebody to run his land for him, and we're gonna do it. We can go fishin' anytime we want in the Arkansas River. You can ride horses all day long, and we can just be ourselves and not have to worry about anybody lookin' over our shoulders or . . . Shit. Boy. I got this planned. This is gonna work. . . . Ain't nobody gonna bother us. Ain't nobody gonna tell me what to do anymore. I'm sick and tired of it. All my life they just . . . break me like a horse. My plans just . . . I got somethin' in me, boy, and they just kill it. I'm sick and tired of your mama treatin' me — sick and tired of my mama and daddy treatin' me like all I do is embarrass them. Bullshit.

One of these days you're gonna know what I'm talkin' about and you're gonna come up to me and say, "Daddy, I wanna thank you for tellin' me the things you told me. Daddy, what you told me was absolutely right. Daddy, I'm glad I listened to you." You're gonna do that to me, Eric. You're gonna tell me that you love me and you're gonna thank me for teachin' you what's right. I ain't gonna make you feel like you can't do nothin' right. Like you can't measure up. I ain't gonna make you feel like you ain't the man you're supposed to be. I ain't gonna hold you back.

THE REST OF THE NIGHT

Robert Lewis Vaughan

Dramatic
Keith, late twenties to early thirties

Keith, the new deputy sheriff, meets Malia for the first time when he's dispatched to inform her that her husband has been arrested. Keith is immediately drawn to Malia, and over time he falls in love with her. Knowing that Miller, Malia's husband, is an alcoholic and possibly a violent one at that, Keith fears for Malia and her son, Eric. Finally, after a particularly bad incident that involved Eric during one of Miller's binges, Keith decides it's time to come clean with Malia.

KEITH: My wife was a partier. Oh boy, she liked her good times. I liked mine to, but . . . She liked hers more. I had as much fun as she did when we'd go out dancin' and drinkin' and raisin' our hell. I'd drink my beers, she'd drink her whiskey sours, and I'd eat her cherries. What the hell, I mean . . . we were nothin' but kids when we first got married and was doin' that. What else was there? It didn't seem like there was too many options for us, that we cared for anyway. So we kept on partyin' and pretendin' that we were fine . . . and, we knew we weren't. Then we started fightin'. I don't have a bad temper. I never did. I just don't have it in me, but she did. She was so hotheaded sometimes that I'd think there was somethin' wrong with her. So. We'd fight and we'd make up, and she'd wanna go play and I'd say no and we'd fight some more, and she'd go by herself and I'd sit home wonderin' what kind of man I was lettin' my wife go off like that. . . .

Things went on like that for a while, and then I got tired of sittin' home when she'd run off. I followed her and I wish I hadn't'a 'cause I didn't like what I found. I loved her to death, Malia, I really did. I couldn't think about any other woman when I was with her. Not like that anyway. I thought I was about the luckiest guy in town, but . . . People started tellin' me I better get a better grip if I was plannin' on keepin' her, so I tried. But we had two different things in mind, and all we started doin' was fightin' more than we ever did and she started cheatin' on me for real. And we had bigger fights — she used to throw things —

boy, I tell you, she had one hell of a good arm. She run outside this last time and she was goin' — I mean she was leavin', and I run out after her and was hell-bent for leather gonna drag her butt back in the house. She was in the car and I run up and dove into the window and tried to get the keys and she's got the damn thing started. She's hittin' me and scratchin' me and bitin' me and . . . she . . . starts backin' up and I don't know what hits me but I slipped and fell . . . she run right over my leg. . . .

Hell, I laugh about it now. What else can I do? It musta looked funny. We had a couple neighbors waterin' their grass standin' around with their mouths plumb hangin' open, not knowin' what the hell to do with me layin' there in the driveway with my leg run over. She was drivin' off down the street callin' me every name in the book and hollerin' back that she hoped it hurt worse than it looked like it did.

ROCKET CITY, ALABAM'

Mark Saltzman

More information on this playwright may be found in the "Meet Our Authors" tab at www.smithandkraus.com.

Dramatic
U.S. Army Major Hamilton Pike Jr., thirty-two

Major Pike is an all-American, Princeton-educated rich boy with political ambitions. The Redstone Missile, the first of the American guided missiles, was designed and built in Rocket City (Hunstville), Alabama. Major Pike is speaking to Amy, a young woman from the Bronx, about exactly what she has been protesting. It's six feet wide. The top of the missile reaches up, up, up, beyond what's visible onstage.

MAJOR PIKE: It's pretty much an adaptation of the V-2. But it's OUR adaptation. Slightly taller, more powerful engine. And what do you think we're calling it, after much consideration, you know what we're naming the baby? We're naming it for this place, for the Redstone Arsenal. This is the Redstone Missile. And soon, when it's launched, the entire world will know about *(In southern dialect.)* the little ol' Redstone Arsenal in little ol' Huntsville, Alabam'. The Germans are about to be naturalized. In a few weeks time you'll be going after American citizens, not foreigners. Can't you just step back and admire what they've done? What they've built here? I mean, just as an object in the world, don't you think it's beautiful? Yes, of course, you can get psychoanalytical about it. But forget that, just think of it as a pure shape, a shape going back to the obelisks of Egypt. Further back! To the prehistoric monoliths still standing in the British Isles. People prayed to those rocket-shaped stones and I bet I know what they were praying for. Protection. And here it is, the answer to an ancient prayer. Our god of war. He has come to earth to protect us because he loves us. It's that tall you know, because most if it is a fuel tank. Everything about it is designed for practicality and physics — a tower of pure function — and yet, look! It turns out to be a thing of beauty. The most ancient of shapes wedded to the most modern technology. And unlike obelisks and monoliths . . . THIS BABY CAN FLY! *(To the missile.)* CAN'T YOU? YES, FLY! And you'll make the most beautiful of trajectories — a perfect parabola, the arching curve of the rainbow, a shape that the Bible tells us was created by God Himself. Look at this thing, Amy — And you plan to stop it? What do you want to do, kick it? Go ahead. It can take it. It can take heat up to two thousand degrees Fahrenheit. Lie down in front of it when it takes off? Chain yourself to it? Instead, why don't we stand together and admire this supersonic masterpiece that will protect our country and take us through that low-lying sky, past the planets, through the Milky Way, past faraway galaxies, to the entrance of whatever heaven is waiting there beyond.

THE ROOKY WOOD
Don Nigro

Dramatic
Hobb, forties

A woman has come to Inspector Ruffing insisting that a girl has been murdered and is lying naked in the woods next to a theater performing Shakespeare in the park. But she can offer no solid evidence except that she has seen the dead girl in a kind of vision. Inspector Ruffing has brought in Hobb for questioning, but Hobb has turned the tables on Ruffing by insisting that he himself is in fact an inspector investigating the murder, and Ruffing is the suspect. At this point, we're not at all sure who to believe.

HOBB: Are you certain? Are you absolutely certain you're not the killer? I'm not certain about anything. That's the beauty of it. All possibilities are open to me. Whereas you, with your closed mind, are a prisoner of your own fabricated realities. You're trapped in a house of mirrors. You lead a very isolated life, don't you? Keeping odd hours. Obsessed with women. It's a wonder we didn't begin to suspect you a long time ago. I wonder if that's it. It's a part of your illness that you commit these murders and then immediately forget them. Then you wake up in the morning and go out and look for the killer. And all the while you're looking for yourself. I don't believe in theories. But if I had to guess how it works, I'd guess something like this: A man goes out in the pouring rain. He has nothing in particular on his mind. He has no plan. He stops under an awning near the park. There's a woman standing there. They strike up a conversation. He's very nice, and not bad looking, and she seems to like him. The man begins to think, perhaps something will come of this. And, after a bit, something does. Or perhaps he meets her at the theater. Or in a police station. It really doesn't matter. But I think it all rather seems each time to have been almost an accident. Of course, it never is an accident. Well, if I were a killer, I don't think I'd just leave my victim lying about with me in the woods. I think I should be tempted to take her home with me and have her embalmed. Some people have difficulty throwing things away. Letting things go. But that also is vanity. Everything goes away. Even embalming is only postponing the inevitable rotting of the flesh. In the end, you must learn to let things go. That is the last thing we learn. To stand under an awning in the rain with a woman who is not unattractive and to become aware, gradually, that something is possible. That something could happen. I imagine it's an extraordinary feeling. We go through our lives half asleep most of the time. And then suddenly, for a moment, something causes us to wake up. To look with new eyes. We realize that time is — that certain moments — that one can, that it is possible to — Suppose a man suddenly became so curious about the mystery of things, he had to see what was inside. He had to see. And there she was, in the rain.

(Pause.)

You look like you could use a drink, Inspector.

ROUGH SKETCH

Shawn Nacol

More information on this playwright may be found in the "Meet Our Authors" tab at www.smithandkraus.com.

Dramatic
Dex, thirties

Dex is speaking to Barbara, a coworker for whom he has strong feelings and with whom he's shared an intense week locked together in the offices of the animation studio that employs them both. A former children's author and recovering alcoholic, Dex has discovered that Barbara plans to sabotage a huge animated family film by rendering a brief sequence with a little heroine's tear in a way that ridicules all family entertainment. In this moment, Dex reveals to Barbara that he has found a way to thwart her disturbing plans.

DEX: I was up here over Christmas weekend so I wouldn't actually lose my shit and spend the day in the bottom of a bottle. Calling my daughter with nothing to say. Pathetic, right? I have another reason. A higher purpose. A heroic task worthy of my skill and experience. Possibly the reason I totaled my whole stupid career! Stopping you. I don't even want a drink! This is BETTER than selling out. You know?! Better than reprint galleys warm in my hands. Barbara, I'm a *drunk* and I wouldn't lick scotch off a nipple if you gave me a hundred million dollars. Imagine! You've tricked Spence. You're going to use his equipment to make him look like a fool. To destroy everything he believes in. That I believe in. That most of the civilized world believes in. You aren't powerful. You aren't scary. But your idea is. I don't have your technical expertise, but I am three million times the artist. Fuck you. I could have helped if you hadn't been a sociopathic nitwit. There are at least thirty places where wittier armature and tinting would've made selecting your sequence inevitable. Imagineering. Polish points where ole Dex could've squirted his finger-licking eyejizz. Fuck you. Your cold, calculating, callous spirit has planted red flags all the hell over your clip that'll nag, nag, nag at Spence and undermine the impact of your tear. Fuck you. I don't need to delete your work, my work will be better, hands down. I'm an artist. Fuck you. Line in the sand! I made a tear.

SLIPPING
Daniel Talbott

Dramatic
Eli, seventeen

Alone, numb, and friendless after the violent death of his father, high school senior Eli has moved with his mother from San Francisco to a fresh start in Iowa. A new relationship with a boy named Jake at school exposes Eli again to the possibility of closeness and the danger of being swallowed by it. Falling back into his old patterns and his self-destructive and physically punishing behavior, Eli attempts to confront his mother, possibly for the last time, about her adultery and her relationship with his father.

ELI: I hated him.
Dad. For being so quiet.
For being so weak.
For not being man enough to keep you.
(Short pause.)
I used to imagine what it must have been like to make love to him.
Sweaty and fat and useless.
(Short pause.)
It makes me sick that I never told him about me.
About Chris.
(Short silence.)
There's that picture of him as a boy. With the beer and the salmon?
I always thought that was my dad.
That was the man you married.
I kept wondering where he went. Where you put him.
(Short pause.)
I never felt like I was any part of you. Like . . .
I never wanted you to be able to take credit for anything I was.
(Silence.)
When he died I kept wishing it was you.
That it'd been you and Roger in the car.
At the funeral I kept trying to guess which picture we'd use.

What you'd wear.
What type of flowers we'd have.
Who would come.
(Beat.)
I'd find these lists that he'd write all over the house.
Like, Eli likes Joy Division. Look it up.
What are Dickies and who is Ani?
Eli mentioned girl. Remember to ask who and does she like movies?
France or London? Which is cooler vacation spot?
Don't put down hair.
Don't be an ass.
Tell him I'm proud.

SMUDGE
Rachel Axler

More information on this playwright may be found in the "Meet Our Authors" tab at www.smithandkraus.com.

Seriocomic
Pete, thirties

Pete is an executive with the census bureau. His brother, who also works at the bureau, has been acting strangely lately due to the recent birth of his horribly deformed daughter. Pete doesn't know about this yet. All he knows is that his brother has been sending out rather demented census questionnaires.

PETE: I said, is there a pig in here? I dunno, you tell me. We got a couple of calls about the new round of surveys. Apparently, someone snuck in a little supplemental. Anything you maybe wanted to mention? Weirdo violent questionnaire, fifty-two, fifty-one . . . Tick-tick, bro. You're wasting my time and yours. And time is money, which is power, which is money, which neither of us is gonna have pretty soon when we both lose our jobs over this, which is why you better start talking in the next two seconds.

One second. Man, swear to crap, I wish we were still kids, so I could beat you up.

(He holds up a copy of the survey.)

It *is* weird. It's, like, gnomes-in-a-cuckoo-clock weird. *And* it's violent, *and* it's no-joke, one-hundred-percent, honest-to-fuck *long*.

(Reading.)

"Would you kill a pig? If yes, continue below. If no, turn to page two. First question! Would you kill a fucking pig?"

"Is it OK for a hog farmer to kill a pig?"

"Have you ever eaten bacon?"

"Are you a vegetarian-slash-Kosher?"

"Have you ever been a member or groupie of a hardcore or thrash metal band?"

Oh, here's a good one. This might be my favorite.

(Reading.)

"Please number the items in the following list from one to twelve, in order of your willingness to kill them, where one is 'most acceptable' and twelve is 'least acceptable.' A pig. A puppy. A roach. A cow. A horsefly. A horse. A dragonfly. A dragon. A baby. A lobster. A celebrity. A stranger."

Well, glad to see Little Nicky lookin' out for numero one, but guess what, bro? *It's not important to the census bureau.* Not on their time and not on their dime. Hey, d'ja hear that? Maybe I should skip this statistics shit and become Poet Fucking Laureate. 'Cause you know, that would be important to *me.*

You're upsetting people. We got complaints from nearly every district about this, people saying they're not gonna return any of the forms, claiming mental aggravation — It's because you're asking them to KILL things. For sixteen fucking pages! Dude.

All we want to know is race, gender, income, dependents, how far do you fucking commute to work? You want to "figure something out" about people's ethos . . . es? Fine! Go. Take some time off, but don't accost an entire city!

Seriously. Toolshed. What is *wrong* with you? This is a fireable offense I gotta cover up here, plus you're slacking on the job, don't think I'm the only one who's noticed, reading fucking psychology books —

And top it all off, Ma's still calling me, trying to reach you, says you dropped off the face of the earth, she's worried you're dead or worse, and I can't help thinking: Is this my fault? Was I that camel who gave my brother a straw to sip from, and then broke his back? 'Cause I gotta say, I'm doubting my choice to give you that presentation now. And I don't like being doubted. Particularly by myself.

SOUL SAMURAI
Qui Nguyen

Comic
Cert, nineteen

Cert, a high-energy b-boy (a break dancer), meets and drops some smooth moves on Dewdrop, a tough-talking Brooklyn girl.

CERT: *(To himself.)* My name is Cert
I'm here to kick it
Don't step to me, boy,
'Cause my shit is wicked
Ninja fly shit is how I be dealin' it
I'm a Samurai, son, so you best be feelin' it

Konichiwa, bozu,
Fuck you up old schoo'
Knock out ya teeth like a Eastside Sifu

Remember these words
Remember my face
I'm the C. E. R. T.
This hood's my place.

Why hello there, fly girl. Yo, baby, did you clean your pants with Windex? 'Cause I can practically see myself in them. My name is Damon. But my homies call me Cert. You can call me anything you want. What's yo' name? Is that Russian? I love Russian chicks.

You don't look Russuan but I'm black and I ain't exactly dark-complected, now am I? My mom's Jewish. But I'm hung like a brotha if you know what I mean . . .

SOUTHERN RAPTURE

Eric Coble

More information on this playwright may be found in the "Meet Our Authors" tab at www.smithandkraus.com.

Seriocomic
Reverend Dupree, forties to fifties, but could be any adult age

> *A local community theater is planning to put on a production of* Rapture in America *(a doppelgänger for* Angels in America*), a controversial play that was a huge hit in New York but which Dupree thinks is inappropriate for the community. Here, he is urging the town's mayor to prohibit the production of the play.*

REVEREND DUPREE: [Your grandfather] . . . he wanted a better life for his wife and five children. Am I rememberin' your stump speech rightly? . . .

So he took that job, the job with the meat store . . . because that was the best he could get. And how did he get through that, what made his life worth livin', what gave him some shred of meaning when he was knee-deep in blood and fat, arteries still seepin' and intestines bustin' . . .

His family and his church! *That's* what kept him going, that's what made his life worth living, the same as for every other soul who's ever lived here or ever will live here. Do you think he would have even thought one second about packin' up his wife and his babies and haulin' 'em to a city that was known for its homosexual parties? Where the people "embraced" naked men having intercourse right in front of children in the public parks? . . .

No, he would not. There are a million more men like your grandfather and father looking at our city right now, and the million more who already live here, who call this home, who go to church every Sunday and pray to God to keep their families intact and their children safe, and Olympics be damned, do you think *any* of them are going to stay here when we put out a big ol' blinkin' sign: "Welcome to New Sodom! Abandon Clothes and Morals All Ye Who Enter Here!"

SOUTHERN RAPTURE

Eric Coble

Dramatic

Winston, forties to fifties, but could be any adult age

A local community theater is planning to put on a production of Rapture in America *(a doppelgänger for* Angels in America*), a controversial play that was a huge hit in New York. This has stirred up a hornet's nest in the town, and local conservative leaders are putting up a big stink about it. Winston, the town's mayor, is caught between a rock and a hard place. He's not really for censorship, but he recognizes that if the theater goes forward with the production, it will hurt his efforts to get the community to support the arts in general, so he has come to the woman who runs the theater to ask her to agree not to open the play.*

WINSTON: I'm askin' you to answer to your fellow citizens! And your fellow artists in this city . . . [who] may have some words for you when we have some words for you when we have to cut all their public funding as well. . . .

. . . [G]overnment can't start gettin' into "oh, this art is good and this art is bad and these guys are OK, but not these" — that's censorship! So we cut nothin' or we cut everything!

. . . [Because] I asked you for one thing — ONE! To do your dirty little epic quietly and you gave me your word — your word, Marjorie — that you would, and is it any wonder now I'm trying to get it in *writing* that you'll clean up your own act??

. . . You don't like what I do, you can have an election. I don't like what you do, I can damn well stop paying for it! And when the symphony and the ballet and the art museum are cuttin' shows and firing staff and shuttin' doors, they are all gonna know to look to the theater who couldn't keep its goddamn prick in its goddamn pants!!

. . . You know how many years we fought to get public funding for the arts? To get people to start appreciating the arts? And now you want to march in here and just undo all that in a single night. If that's what happens, it's on your head. Not mine. Yours.

(Beat.) This document is just asking you to *think,* Marjorie. To think about where you are and when you are and who you are and to use a little common-sense discretion. *(He pushes the paper toward her.)*

You sign this and I can go to the yellers outside and tell 'em they can rest easy and go home. That you've learned your lesson. And the world can stop laughing at us. *(He holds up a pen.)* Please.

SUICIDE, INCORPORATED

Andrew Hinderaker

More information on this playwright may be found in the "Meet Our Authors" tab at www.smithandkraus.com.

Dramatic
Jason, twenty-five

Jason works for Legacy Letters, a start-up company that edits their clients' suicide notes. A new hire, Jason is determined to save his clients. Here, Jason is speaking to Norm, a lonely and desperate man who hired Jason to write his suicide note. Jason, who is guilt-ridden over his role in his brother's death and his inability to dissuade his clients from killing themselves, has decided to take his own life. After trying repeatedly and desperately to save Norm's life, Jason — in this moment — asks Norm to save his own.

JASON: We'll get in the car — And, and we'll drive to this place where I volunteer. And they'll see me and say, "I didn't know you had a shift tonight," and I'll say "I don't" and then that'll sink and then they'll say . . . "*Oh.*" And then we'll go to the waiting room, and we'll probably wait like an hour 'cause there's only one counselor on call. And when it's finally our turn, we'll both walk up there, and they'll tell us they typically see one person at a time, and I'll say you've been paying me to write your suicide note, so it's not exactly a typical situation. And then we'll go in, and you'll listen to me talk for a bit, and then if you want, you'll talk for a bit, and maybe that'll help and maybe it won't. And then we'll take off. And by then it'll almost be morning, and if it's OK, we'll drive out to this breakfast place I know in the hills. I used to take my brother there after he'd pulled an all-nighter — and see, the thing is I used to ride him about his schoolwork — I used to ride him so fucking hard . . . But then I'd take him to this place for breakfast . . . And it was so nice 'cause you're up there in the hills and — God, I'd almost forgotten about this, you know? I mean, he loved this 'cause if you get there early enough, and I think — you and me — I think we'll get there while it's still dark. And see, if you get there early — the haze, it comes up over the hills and it just covers this place. I mean, in an instant, everywhere you look, it's just *white.* And we'll sit up there, you and me, right by the window, and we'll look out and we won't be able to see a thing. So we'll just sit there. And eat our breakfast. Drink our coffee. And after a little while, the haze'll start to — I mean, there's no sunrise, nothing big like that. After the way the haze comes in, you expect some, like, break of day, but it's not, it just . . . It just gets a little lighter. And that's all you get to let you know the night's over.

THAT PRETTY PRETTY; OR, THE RAPE PLAY

Sheila Callaghan

More information on this playwright may be found in the "Meet Our Authors" tab at www.smithandkraus.com.

Dramatic

Owen, twenties

Owen, a slacker type, stares into a mirror. He dons a long evening gown and takes a deep cleansing breath. He addresses himself.

OWEN: Come on, Owen. Get into it. SLUT SUPREME.

(He opens a makeup bag and begins applying makeup, facing forward.)

I am so fucking pretty. I am so fucking fucking pretty, yo. Suckass. You wanna suck lemons from my cheeks. I got fuckin' mad pretty on my shit. My pretty is like PROFOUND. It has emissions. Waves of pretty. I'm like a gas burner of pretty. Stick a pot on me, I'll make it whistle. Step the fuck off, right, 'cause my pretty will eat your soul. My pretty is a black hole. I am so pretty I drain all the ugly off you and wear it like a swimsuit. GODDAMN AM I PRETTY. Holy fucking shit. You can't stand it. You are like, she is so pretty I need to BASH her. I need to tear her pubes out. I need to hate on her. That pretty is cancerous. That pretty is a little iced cookie and I need to bite it. That pretty is TOXIC. That pretty boils in my gut, it eats me up, that pretty comes to me at night and scrapes all my tender spots. Soils my boxer briefs. That pretty is FUCKED UP, I need to poke through it with my thumbs, I need to fuck the joy out of that pretty. I want to kill that pretty. I want to kill that pretty. I want to kill that pretty. That's what they say about me.

THAT PRETTY PRETTY; OR, THE RAPE PLAY

Sheila Callaghan

Seriocomic
Owen, twenties

Owen, a slacker type, is in a hotel room talking to his best friend, Rodney. He's pitching his screenplay idea.

OWEN: OK. So like, there's the two chicks. They're like sisters. Or half-sisters. They tell everyone that. And they are SO FUCKING HOT. So hot that like, your eyebrows get singed around them. Like too hot. And rude. So rude that you like have to put them into a condom. I mean they are SICK. Heavy shit, these two. And one is a bulimic. And the other is. I dunno. Puerto Rican or something. A real bulldog. Smart, ballsy. Doesn't take shit. One's a secret lezzy. The PR. AND, she's been fucking the bulimic's husband since they were sixteen. And they do coke off each other's asses in front of some businessmen. At a dinner party. They're strippers. EX-strippers. The PR girl got fucked over by the two businessmen, which is why she hates men so bad. Which is why she's fucking her sister's husband. Because she secretly hates him too. He has a back problem and a bowel problem. He has to wear a diaper. He fucks her because (a) she's SICK hot, and (b) he feels bad for her. Because she has jaundice. Ho, wait. Hepatitis, not jaundice. I get them confused. So like, then she accuses the husband of raping her, which is how the bulimic finds out they were fucking. There was no fucking rape. YET. But like, OK, so here's the meat: One night PR is on the pole, right? And she's workin' it. Good night, bachelor party up front, Japanese suits in the back . . . In walks Bulimia. And Bulimia's got this LOOK on her face, like a little . . .

(Owen trembles his bottom lip. Girl voice:)

"Our baby sister got capped," she says. "Some neo-con stuffed his trunk full of shit and drove up outside this clinic. BOOOOM. They found part of her hanging from a telephone pole three blocks away. So they stand there, and they DON'T EVEN CRY. No crying. Not even a whimper. DIGNITY SUPREME. The PR just kind of turns to the camera and looks us dead in the eye and says, "IT'S ON." So PR's like the mastermind of the whole enterprise. She (a) makes the blog, (b) gets the camera, and (c) buys the gun. She writes this long-ass manifesto — all this shit about her uterus, the Internet, the FCC, et cetera. They pool all their stripper money together and procure a hoopty. They motor from state to state and show up to all these pro-life conventions looking like Grade A Tail. They bring home the sloppy dudes. Fuck 'em if they can get wood. And THEN.

(Owen makes gun-fingers and pulls the trigger)

BANG! *(Girl voice.)* "Keep your laws off my fucking body!" There's TOTALLY a market for this shit! These bitches with the blog, they're like female Dukes of Hazzard. Taking the law into their own hands. *(Girl voice.)* "Don't fuck with me suckass or I will cut you!" I already have a title. "An Unbearable Proposition." And there's more! So one night they're in Mississippi at this convention. Everything is swell. Dude's getting sloppy, spilling Wild Turkey on his pants. They make the transaction. PR goes to her car to get change. Dude follows her out and BEATS THE LIVING CRAP OUT OF HER. I mean she is TOTALLY fucked up. Black eye, lip hanging. But of course she looks so fucking hot. So she's there in the hospital, all fucked up and hot. And THEN there's rape. Lots of it. The orderly rapes the PR. And then the doctor. And then a male nurse. It's one big bang-fest. And the dudes feel fucking AWFUL about it. But the PR lezzy NEVER FUCKING CRIES. She stands all shakey and bloody and dignified with her chin turned up, and then the doctor who was the last to have her — he can't look her in the face, because this is like his greatest downfall, he's like "Tragically Flawed Dude," hubris and all that, he's like Hamlet, right, and he thinks about how in med school they never prepared you for the fuckable lost ones, you know the ones who don't actually look into your eyes but through you as if you were a pile of ash because of all the fucked-up ruinous shit from their past, a molestey stepdad or white slavery or whatever, so they gotta exact some foul revenge on you because you are (a) in the way and (b) looking like someone who needs to be taken down, and so they spread their damage on a shiny silver platter and say "munch it, baby," and you just can't stop yourself because nothing tastes more delicious than a steaming hot mound of damage. So the doctor is thinking this shit, and then he thinks of his wife at home and his two sons, they're twins and they wear matching baseball pajamas to bed, and his wife lost all the baby weight the second they popped out because she didn't want to be one of those lard asses in the Key Foods wearing sweatpants and a hairnet, and like she never leaves the house without makeup, and all his golf buddies are like "how the fuck did YOU land such a tasty beverage," and he gets fake-mad at them, but he is secretly so fucking proud because he's the only one of them who still gets regular blowjobs, and when he goes home that night she'll be waiting for him on the porch drinking a glass of white wine and smoking a jay, and she'll offer him a hit and ask him how his day was, and at that moment — AT THAT MOMENT he'll conjure that bloody fucking broken cunty bitch in her little hospital gown and her eyes made of ash and he will release her into the evening air and she will never enter his mind again. So this neurosurgeon is finishing up his rape, and he's pulling up his scrubs and thinking about his wife and not looking at PR, and PR tries to say something all significant like a supreme-like philosophical sentence or whatever, but he whispers "just go." And walks out. And she's left there alone in the room. And she stands up all wobbly on her colt legs, and her hospital gown is all open and you can see her titties, and then Bulimia shows up. And she looks at PR, all fucked up and raped. And she's like, wait a second. I'm still sore about PR fucking my husband. But what she DOESN'T know is — get this — is that PR fucked her husband to get the cash for their baby sister's abortion! And Bulimia DOESN'T KNOW! So Bulimia steps out of the room to quote-unquote "get a Diet Coke," and comes back with a gat. BAM. Never saw her coming. Um wait. She's not blind. She's just normal.

(He types a little)

And dykey. A little dykey. Wears dresses and thongs but likes to fuck girls. Some fucked-up shit chicks go through. Rape, and babies, and stripping, and being objectified by the media . . . I want to write a movie my mom will be proud of. My mom is a strong fucking woman, homes. Every time one of her ex-husbands dumps on her, she takes it like a pro. Chin up. Pure class. Tablecloths and linens. That's my mom. She's my hero, man. And you know who her hero is?

(Points to TV.)

Hanoi. Fucking. Jane.

THE THIRD STORY
Charles Busch

More information on this playwright may be found in the "Meet Our Authors" tab at www.smithandkraus.com.

Seriocomic
Drew, twenties to thirties

Drew is a failed Hollywood screenwriter in the 1940s. He's been trying very hard to maintain his independence from his flamboyant screenwriter mother. Toward the end of the play and in this monologue, Drew gives up and reveals to his mother just how overwhelming his love is for her.

DREW: Mother, I've got a story for you. A scorcher. . . .

Three years ago when I got that phone call that you'd been in the car accident, I drove to the hospital and found you in that horrible trauma room. There was still blood in your hair. They told me you were going to die, and this wave of intense panic swept over me. What would happen to me if you were gone? How could I exist in a world without you? Well, I had to be admitted to the hospital too. The psychiatric wing . . .

After I left you, I started going buggy and was wandering around downtown muttering to myself in a way that was making a lot of people extremely nervous. I don't remember any of this, but evidently, I walked into a department store and ended up in the ladies try-on room. I guess I reverted back to when I was a little kid and you took me in there with you to get my opinion. The police came and carted me off to the mental ward . . .

And then it just went away. By the time you came out of the coma, I was strong enough to take care of you. . . .

I know I've been awful to you. I gripe and moan and accuse you of every crime against humanity. And what's the point? Some sort of half-hearted stab at independence? I moved all the way to Nebraska to get away from you. Well, I give up. You're the most fascinating person I'll ever know. I should just accept my fate and enjoy it. I'll go back to Los Angeles with you . . .

I'm completely on the level. We always have fun together. I don't know why I'm forever trying to fight it. And I'll work on this outline with you. I can see the whole thing. Truly. The zombie, the lady scientist . . . the mob queen. And she won't be a grotesque harridan like the mother in my play. The mob queen will have all sorts of color and shadings. The mother in our movie will be a portrait you can be proud of. Let's keep going. Where were we?

TROJAN BARBIE

Christine Evans

More information on this playwright may be found in the "Meet Our Authors" tab at www.smithandkraus.com.

Seriocomic
Mica, twenties to thirties

Mica is a soldier from Troy, New York, who's been on tour far too long. He's a modern version of the eternal soldier — working class, sick of his job, adrift in time. In ancient times, he'd have been one of Odysseus's companions, trudging through different lands as the dream of home recedes. Here, he could be on his third repeat tour of Iraq. Mica has been assigned to local spin, guarding the women's camp, where he's met Helen of Troy, whom he adores. Here, he addresses the people (audience) who line up outside the wire, waiting for visas, food, water — until his own longing takes him elsewhere.

MICA: As I was saying. We regret any casualties and the loss of innocent life. Humanitarian priorities are high on our list. I ask for your patience with the monumental changes we are installing. Rome wasn't burned in a day. Built. Rome wasn't built in a day.

Now, progress can be slow. But action isn't everything. It's being *prepared* for action that matters. Now that takes discipline, hanging round day after day waiting for something to happen. The main event here is, the latrines overflow. That gets pretty exciting. A homemade tattoo gets infected. A bird lands looking for water. Or someone tries to hang herself in the tent. Then there's the moaning and wailing. We let that pass, but we discourage the singing. Singing could lead to action.

But there's no action.

Any English speakers out there today?

— Fuck.

Well. These long tours of duty, it's all about survival. Two simple rules:

One: Compartmentalize.

Two: Cover your ass.

For instance, number one. Managing downtime. Well, there's Helen. Fifty-seven percent of people meet their partners through work. And I've got a stack of magazines, and I worked out how to link the satellite phone to the nine hundred numbers back home. That helps, a little. Knowing that the world's still out there.

Man, I just can't wait to be back home in Troy, New York.

Walk down to the canal, past that big old statue of Uncle Sam.

Past the old factories and new real estate offices.

Taste real beer again.

Play pool with the guys on Friday and lose half my paycheck.

If any of them are still there.

Not much action back home either, with the steelworks finished and half of us enlisted. After ten years away, you're like a ghost, haunting the streets of your own fucking life.

Maybe when I get home, I'll just get a big black Humvee with the windows all blacked out. Tear up the map and head West. Drive for three days 'til I hit the ocean and then just keep on going. Man, I've got so much grit in my eyes, they feel like they've been sandpapered. Feel like the whole of the Desert Storm happened right inside my eyeballs. I'm gonna wash them clean with blue, blue water. Let the sand slide away, and the road, and the dry grit that coats your skin and gets in every crack.

I'll just step on the gas and drive into the wide blue smile of the sea.

Helen makes me think of the sea.

And after the first jolt as you hit the water, everything slows down
real smooth and peaceful.

Fish swim past the windshield.

Maybe a lazy old shark will turn his head to say hello.

Seals. Seaweed.

An old submarine blows bubbles at you from some long-forgotten war,
growing barnacles and leaking poison into the sea.

And slowly you sink down into the green
then the blue
then the inky darkness
where only the giant squids live, blind and harmless.
They won't bother you, and no, they're not winking
it's just a trick of the last little dribble of light.

After a while the barnacles will build a home on the roof.

A few more years, and the little fish swim through your eye sockets
to hide from the sharks in the back of your skull.

Still "protecting the weak" even here.

— Jesus.

Maybe Helen will move out West with me.

THE UNDERSTUDY
Theresa Rebeck

Comic
Harry, thirties to forties

Harry is an actor who has been hired to understudy a film star in a Broadway production of a recently discovered lost play by Kafka. Occasionally, he addresses the audience directly, as he does here, talking about what an incoherent way acting is to make a living.

HARRY: I know a lot of people who say we're crazy. Crazy actors! Don't date an actor, they're crazy! And I'm not actually in any position to argue that, given my personal history. My financial situation. The fact that I actually had to change my name, we don't need to get into why that happened, but it's not actually a story that recommends acting as a sensible profession. I mean, it's great being an actor, when you get to do it, but it's also incoherent. Incoherent is the right word honestly, it's really not, as I think it's clear, it's not a mature choice in a lot of ways. But you know I worked in an office once. I was a temp? So I was doing temp things, answering phones, typing up memos, and then for a while they had me adding numbers all day. Seriously, I sat in this cubicle with a little adding machine and tapped in these numbers, I can't remember why, but periodically this woman, her name was Jane something, would come by my cubicle and just scream at me! Literally hold out slips of paper, and she would be in an utter rage and I would think what what what? And it would be nothing. A number in the wrong place. One time I typed up a memo on the wrong color paper. Like that. So I know people think people who work in the theater are crazy? But I'm not so sure we're any worse than the rest of you.

THE UNSEEN

Craig Wright

Dramatic
Wallace, could be any age

Imprisoned by a totalitarian regime and mercilessly tortured for unknown crimes, Wallace lives without hope of escape or release. His only human contact, other than his subhuman torturers, is an inmate in a nearby cell named Valdez. Wallace is paranoid and semidelusional, as he demonstrates here.

WALLACE: You could be hypnotized or programmed or somehow surgically altered, Mister Valdez, and you could be taking everything in that I say and do without even realizing it, and you could be painstakingly, unconsciously recording it in a secret sector of your brain hidden even from you, Mister Valdez — even from you. And then, when they take you to the room for treatment, they could activate that secret sector of your brain with a signatory word, for instance, or an electrode, or a pulsing electromagnetic device of some sort, and thus make you talk and divulge the contents of that secret sector of your brain that is hidden even from you, Mister Valdez — even from you. And then, once they'd extracted the information, they could close the doors once more, and darken the long cerebral hallways leading to that secret sector of your brain hidden even from you, Mister Valdez, even from you — and then they'd sweetly send you back here to continue sponging up the messy information that's continuously dripping from my mouth. In this manner, you could be a spy and you would not even know it. That's the key. That's the crux. That's the nut. That's the thing. It's impossible, absolutely impossible, to know.

THE UNSEEN

Craig Wright

Dramatic
Wallace, could be any age

Imprisoned by a totalitarian regime and mercilessly tortured for unknown crimes, Wallace lives without hope of escape or release. His only human contact, other than his subhuman torturers, is an inmate in a nearby cell named Valdez. Wallace is paranoid and semidelusional, as he demonstrates here.

WALLACE: I'm exactly the opposite. I feel those are moments of great clarity. It's the rest of my life that's confusing. The point is, from all these details and sensations and impressions, I have meticulously quilted together an absolutely uninterrupted fabric of conclusions, first and foremost of which is this: this prison, Mister Valdez, is structured like an immense, elaborate beehive. The world as we know it has a few basic structures in it, Mister Valdez — a few basic structures that evolution has generated by chance, but which have proven their power over time to perform certain tasks in the ongoing work of making and maintaining reality as it continues to wetly unfold like water, and then like flannel, and then like flesh, and then slowly but surely like crystals and iron as it concretizes into the visible material facts of physical history. Agreed? Provisionally? The symmetrical structure of the snowflake, for instance, or the structure of the vertebrate spine, for instance, all men and women of reason agree these can be taken at this point as givens in this world — as can be the honeycombed structure of the beehive as nature's primary model for housing a multiplicitous population of discrete individuals in the smallest possible space. Witness the coliseum. Witness the skyscraper. Witness the ever-spreading structure of the modern megalopolis. We, as a species, are building ourselves, and have been since the beginning of time, a beehive.

THE UNSEEN
Craig Wright

Dramatic
Smash, could be any age

Smash is a guard at a prison run by a totalitarian regime. He is telling two prisoners, whom he regularly tortures, about how he himself is tortured by feelings of empathy for the tortured.

SMASH: Every morning I wake up and I tell myself I'm not gonna get drawn in. I tell myself, today, I'm just gonna come to work and do my job. But then I get here and — I don't know what happens, I see your faces and I get drawn in! I was thinking last night, laying in bed, we should just take out all your fucking eyes. It would make everything simpler. So I wouldn't have to see what you were thinking all the time! So I wouldn't have to know you were always in, you know, pain! So I spent a few minutes last night, you know, just thinking out loud in bed with my wife, trying to design a little machine that would, you know, remove people's eyes? Something simple we could maybe run people through when they first come in? I figured maybe I could design it, maybe show it to the people in charge, maybe make an impression, you know, get ahead? Don't worry, I'm not going to. Because then I realized, even if we took out your eyes . . . ? You'd still be able to let people know what you were thinking all the time, only then just with words, but I'd still be stuck knowing. All the time, knowing. I HATE IT!

UNUSUAL ACTS OF DEVOTION
Terrence McNally

More information on this playwright may be found in the "Meet Our Authors" tab at www.smithandkraus.com.

Dramatic
Chick, thirties to forties

Chick and Leo have congregated on the rooftop of their Greenwich Village apartment building with other residents to celebrate the fifth wedding anniversary of a couple, Leo and Nadine, who also live there. Chick is a gay, alcoholic tour guide.

CHICK: Stop right there. I'm not always the happiest camper on the planet but I'm not the person you think I am. I have friends. Not as many as you, maybe, but enough. I have a job I love. My evaluation said my joy in my work was infectious! Well, why not? I'm good at what I do. I can tell you anything about Manhattan you want to know. Ask me where Edna Saint Vincent Millay lived . . .

Go on, ask me! . . .

Seventy-five and a half Bedford Street! She was the first woman to win the Pulitzer Prize for poetry. You walk by her house every day on your way to your club, but you didn't know that, did you? . . .

And when was the last time you were in my apartment? Have you seen how I repainted it? I had the sofa recovered in a very bold plaid. I've got a new bed on order. One of those foam ones they advertise on television. You sink into it, and within a week it fits the shape of your body, so it's like your own customized bed. I travel. I'm going to Thailand on my next vacation. I'm going to have my picture taken on an elephant in front of the Royal Palace. I'll send you a postcard. I read, I cook, I vote in every election, even the ones that don't count, what are they called? Primaries! I was a good son to both my parents, and I'm a good sibling to my sister, even though I can't stand her. I'm healthy, I've got my hair, and I'm very glad to be alive at this particular moment in the history of the human race. Is that your profile of a sad and lonely man, Leo? It's not mine.

SCENES

CREATURE
Heidi Schrek

Dramatic
John, thirties to forties
Father Thomas, thirties to forties

John is a brewer whose wife, Margery, has decided to try and become a living saint, which has not only interfered with their marriage but has led to whispers that, in fact, Margery is a Lollard (a heretic). Here, John demands that Father Thomas do something about his wife's eccentric behavior. (Note: A backslash [/] indicates where the next line of dialogue overlaps the current one.)

(Father Thomas's cell. John is holding a bottle of beer. He is a little tipsy.)

JOHN: I brought you our newest beer.

FATHER THOMAS: Thank you.

JOHN: Let's share the bottle.

(Beat.)

FATHER THOMAS: All right.

(Father Thomas opens the bottle and passes it to John. John takes a drink.)

JOHN: How's your life at St. James?

FATHER THOMAS: It's well.

JOHN: You have a Christ-like love for all those smelly beggars?

FATHER THOMAS: Actually, yes.

JOHN: In my opinion, the priests up there are a gang of pirates who steal from the poor.

FATHER THOMAS: Ah.

JOHN: I know I'm just a brewer, but in my view the church is overstepping when it comes to indulgences — I can say that to you right? There are rumors that you're bit of a . . . *free thinker.*

FATHER THOMAS: I support the church and the true Pope.

JOHN: Do you? That's not what they say at the Guildhall.

FATHER THOMAS: I don't pay much attention to idle tongues.

JOHN: Oh yes those of us who work for a living have idle tongues while you priests slave in service to God. Cheers.

FATHER THOMAS: I thought the men at the Guildhall spent all their time getting drunk while the poor slaved in service to *them*. Did you brew that beer with your own hands, John?

JOHN: I work taking care of my son because my wife is too busy loving God to love her family.

FATHER THOMAS: Did you want to discuss something specific?

JOHN: Tell my wife she has to stop wearing white.

FATHER THOMAS: You know that Margery does as she pleases.

JOHN: The whole town is laughing at her.

FATHER THOMAS: I'll speak with her but —

JOHN: She's not married to Jesus Christ she's married to me!

FATHER THOMAS: You need to be patient with her, John.

JOHN: Why? Why the hell should I be patient? Jesus Christ in *purple robes*?

FATHER THOMAS: I believe her.

JOHN: Why?

FATHER THOMAS: I've seen her tears.

JOHN: Obviously you don't have much experience with women.

FATHER THOMAS: John /

JOHN: She's slippery! She's a little snake! When I first met Margery, I thought, this girl is the most gorgeous thing God ever put on this earth, but I never thought she was *honest*!

FATHER THOMAS: She is honest.

JOHN: No! She's a woman and she's beautiful and that's not the same thing. For God's sakes, look deep into your heart Father.

FATHER THOMAS: I look deep into my heart every day, John.

JOHN: And what do you see when you look in there? Some fucking woman! / The problem with women is they don't have to be honest because they're beautiful! They are aren't they? Aren't they? Come on, Father, confess that you think women are beautiful!

FATHER THOMAS: Please stop blaspheming.

JOHN: They're just so — Aaaaaaaaaaaaaaah. They're incredible! With their tits and their /

FATHER THOMAS: John /

JOHN: tits! Oh God and their skin and their soft little —

FATHER THOMAS: Please.

JOHN: What? Does it excite you too much? Is it painful to keep those vows when you hear of other men's exploits?

FATHER THOMAS: Actually, my mother is in the next room.

JOHN: Oh. *(Beat.)* Sorry.

FATHER THOMAS: And I don't like to hear of Margery talked about in that way. She's much more to me — .

JOHN: *(Whispering.)* Much more to *you*? What do you think she is to me? And you've stolen her from me and turned her into the most boring woman on earth.

FATHER THOMAS: Your wife is not boring.

JOHN: Oh no. She isn't? Weeping all day, refusing to eat with me, refusing to fuck me. Jumping out of bed in the middle of night to explain how merry life in heaven is!

FATHER THOMAS: KEEP YOUR VOICE DOWN.

(Beat.)

JOHN: Sorry. *(Resentfully.)* Do you like the beer?

FATHER THOMAS: It's quite good actually.

JOHN: *(Softening.)* There's a bit of a burn but — thank you. This is the first good batch we've had all year. We might have to close the business — we're nearly bankrupt.

FATHER THOMAS: I'm sorry to hear that.

JOHN: Don't be polite — I know the whole town is gossiping about how demons have gotten into our horses, how God is punishing us. Whores / on the street scream "Witch!" when she walks outside /

FATHER THOMAS: You need to be more careful with your —

JOHN: and we've had five men quit because she makes the workers pray and preaches to them in the evenings.

FATHER THOMAS: You have to tell her to stop preaching. It's against the law.

JOHN: She knows it's against the law and she doesn't care! And now her bitch friend /

FATHER THOMAS: John

JOHN: Anne is telling all her other bitch friends that she's a Lollard.

FATHER THOMAS: What?

JOHN: Sorry. I know. I do penance for it every week.

(Beat.)

FATHER THOMAS: She's not a Lollard.

JOHN: No, she's my wife!

FATHER THOMAS: Who's saying that she's a —

JOHN: Everybody! She's got no friends left! She runs around babbling about the music of heaven.

FATHER THOMAS: Has anyone accused her, though? I mean officially.

JOHN: What?

FATHER THOMAS: They just burned a man for being a Lollard.

JOHN: Where? In France?

FATHER THOMAS: No! Nearby — in Smithfield. The bishops are rounding up Lollards —

JOHN: My father-in-law was the mayor. No one's going to burn his daughter.

FATHER THOMAS: William Sautre was a chaplain. They don't care who her father was.

JOHN: Oh, calm down, Father.

FATHER THOMAS: Have you ever smelled burning human flesh?

JOHN: No, but I hear it smells like pork.

FATHER THOMAS: John.

JOHN: It's 1401. They don't burn women anymore!

FATHER THOMAS: The law makes no exception for women.

(Beat.)

JOHN: Then stop teaching her things.

FATHER THOMAS: What?

JOHN: Did you tell her she could wear white?

FATHER THOMAS: Not exactly.

JOHN: And those sermons she's preaching, does she get them from you?

FATHER THOMAS: I don't know. I read to her.

(Beat.)

JOHN: Have you got children?

FATHER THOMAS: What? No. Of course not.

JOHN: And you're going to heaven, right?

FATHER THOMAS: I hope so.

JOHN: So it's not so terrible if they burn you.

(Beat.)

FATHER THOMAS: I'll talk to her about the way she dresses.

JOHN: Good. You can come by the house to do that. She doesn't come here.

FATHER THOMAS: . . . I understand.

JOHN: Thank you. *(Beat.)* Can I ask you another question?

FATHER THOMAS: Yes.

JOHN: Is it true that priests have extra large . . . merchandise?

FATHER THOMAS: Are you drunk?

JOHN: There was some priest I heard about recently from Worms! He was screwing a married woman, driving / her insane. It's not only the size of your wares, it's that they have a special shape.

FATHER THOMAS: All right

FATHER THOMAS: Good night and thank you for the beer.

JOHN: I'm not that drunk!

FATHER THOMAS: I'll speak to Margery about the way she dresses.

JOHN: *(With real gratitude.)* Thank you. Thank you, Father. I love her.

FATHER THOMAS: I know you do.

JOHN: I love her, Father. You care about her eternal soul, but I love her here on earth.

FATHER THOMAS: I understand.

JOHN: You talk with her.

FATHER THOMAS: I will.

JOHN: Thank you. Thank you.

(John hugs Father Thomas tightly then lets him go.)

FATHER THOMAS: I do know that women are beautiful, John.

(John grabs Father Thomas.)

JOHN: Stay the hell away from my wife or we'll chase you out of Lynn with torches. I can do it, Father. They respect me. I'm a respected man.

DREAMTIME

Maura Campbell

More information on this playwright may be found in the "Meet Our Authors" tab at www.smithandkraus.com.

Dramatic
Willy, seventeen
Noah, seventeen

Willy Ranger is checking out a Nazi recruitment website when his friend Noah Stone enters with a special delivery box containing two military-style knives, and they begin to plot their way out of small-town boredom.

WILLY: You in or you out?

NOAH: I don't know.

WILLY: They'd have to approve you, anyway.

NOAH: Who's going to approve you?

WILLY: You're kidding, right? I'm perfect. I'm white —

NOAH: I'm white —

WILLY: I'm English and German, the operative word being German. You're Irish as evidenced by the way your old man gets drunk on St. Paddy's day, not to mention Monday, Tuesday —

NOAH: What if they want you to kill someone?

WILLY: They're not monsters. Look, read what it says, "We are not monsters." I just want the training.

NOAH: Well . . . *(He takes a box out of his backpack.)* You can start with this.

WILLY: They came?

NOAH: Special delivery.

WILLY: Let's have it! *(Willy rips open the box. He takes out two large knives.)* That's what I'm talking about!

NOAH: Wow. I didn't realize they would be so big.

WILLY: Man, I can think of more than one person I'd like to show this to! You know, like the entire student council!

NOAH: These are serious.

(Willy slowly removes his knife from its sheath. He feels the edge of the knife with his thumb.)

WILLY: Worth every penny. What's the matter?

(He takes out two Velcro bands, gives one to Noah and puts the other on his leg. Then he puts the knife inside.)

NOAH: Nothing.

WILLY: Don't you like them?

NOAH: Sure I do. I just think they're kind of big. Heavy, you know?

WILLY: Look, we studied this. We spent hours picking them out.

NOAH: I know, I know. It's fine. It's just on the computer screen they looked different. I was just kind of surprised.

WILLY: Wait a minute, wait a minute. Check this out. *(He walks around.)* Now that is hot. Go on. Tell me if you can see it.

(Willy walks around. Noah laughs.)

WILLY: What?

NOAH: I don't know, you're walking kind of funny.

WILLY: There's nothing funny about having a knife like this on you. *(Beat.)* I don't like being laughed at.

NOAH: Hey. I'm just fooling around. I never know with you. I never know when you're acting serious.

WILLY: What?

NOAH: Nothing.

WILLY: Hey, I am just messing with you.

NOAH: It doesn't feel like it.

WILLY: I got something for you. *(Willy opens his backpack.)* Early Christmas present.

(He hands Noah a folder. Noah opens it.)

NOAH: Is this the chemistry test?

WILLY: No. That's the chemistry answer sheet.

NOAH: Jesus, Willy! How did you get this?

WILLY: Very carefully. Actually, it was just lying on Mr. Prescott's desk. So . . . I picked it up.

NOAH: Won't he miss it?

WILLY: Maybe. But so what? He knows the answers. He's been giving tests for a hundred years.

NOAH: You're saving my life.

WILLY: What do you want to do this weekend? Besides memorize that thing.

NOAH: I don't know. My sister's home for Thanksgiving.

WILLY: Uh-huh. The Jacobs are out of town.

NOAH: So?

WILLY: So I'm thinking maybe we'll hang out at their house. I've got a key.

NOAH: Did you ask them?

WILLY: I work for them! I would just say we were checking on the place. Come on, Noah. The hot tub. The big screen.

NOAH: *(Excited.)* The bar . . .

WILLY: The bar . . . Sarah and Kelsey . . . Hey, let's try these out. You know the Miller's dog?

NOAH: Yeah? What?

WILLY: Let's get it.

NOAH: What are you talking about?

WILLY: It's old. It can barely walk.

NOAH: I'm not killing a dog.

WILLY: Look, we have to know what these can do. In case we ever need them.

NOAH: I'm not killing a dog, Willy!

WILLY: All it does is bark. *(Beat.)* Jesus, Noah! I'm just kidding. I'm just testing you. Come on, you think I'd kill a dog? Lighten up.

NOAH: I've got to go to the store.

WILLY: I feel like climbing. God, it's so claustrophobic in this town! Let's go to Burlington.

NOAH: My mom has to make the stuffing —

WILLY: OK, look, I just need to pick something up. We'll be back in two hours. When does she need to make the stuffing? Thanksgiving's not until tomorrow!

NOAH: She's — I don't know, I'm supposed to get the celery —

WILLY: Fuck it. Let's go to the gym.

NOAH: Fuck it. I'm going to the store.

WILLY: We're climbing. Then we're going to the store.

FARRAGUT NORTH

Beau Willimon

More information on this playwright may be found in the "Meet Our Authors" tab at www.smithandkraus.com.

Dramatic
Stephen, midtwenties
Paul, midforties

Paul is the campaign manager for a presidential candidate. Stephen is the press secretary. The campaign is floundering, and Stephen has just done something really stupid — or has he? (Note: A backslash [/] indicates where the next line of dialogue overlaps the current one.)

(The main terminal at the Des Moines Airport. Stephen is waiting nervously. Paul approaches him from behind, pulling his roll-away suitcase.)

PAUL: Boo!

(Stephen whips around, startled.)

STEPHEN: Paul.

(Paul sets his suitcase aside, pulls a tin of chewing tobacco out of his back pocket, and wedges some chew in his cheek.)

PAUL: Been fucking *dying* the last six hours. Rude to spit into a cup when someone's sittin next to you. I need to find another addiction is what I need to do. This snow — we circled so many times I thought they were gonna reroute us to fuckin' Omaha. How long you been waiting?

STEPHEN: Couple of hours.

PAUL: Sorry you had to wait.

STEPHEN: Don't worry about it.

PAUL: Nice of you to come out here and pick me up. I coulda gotten a cab, you know.

STEPHEN: Well I got a rental this morning, so . . .

PAUL: I hope not an expensive one.

STEPHEN: On my own dime.

PAUL: You shouldn'tve done that. If you needed a car we could've —

STEPHEN: We need to talk.

PAUL: You're sounding way too serious.

STEPHEN: What'd Thompson say?

PAUL: Cocksucker said he's having second thoughts.

STEPHEN: Fuck.

PAUL: I know. Thought this trip was to seal it, but I get to his house this morning, and he starts throwin' up smoke right and left, says he wants to see how things pan out in Iowa. I almost rip him a new asshole, but I stop myself. I ask him — why'd you have me fly all the way out here just to tell me you're not sure? He says he needs more info — what our strategy is over the next ten days, all this shit.

STEPHEN: Did you tell him?

PAUL: Course I told him. Talked his ear off for an hour — exactly how we're gonna take Iowa, every single fucking step. And *still* no dice.

STEPHEN: This is bad Paul.

PAUL: What is?

STEPHEN: Thompson's not gonna endorse.

PAUL: He's just playin' a little hard to get.

STEPHEN: No Paul — he's definitely not gonna endorse.

PAUL: What are you talking about?

STEPHEN: He's gonna endorse Pullman three days out. Fuck — I should have called you last night, but I was hoping it wasn't true. I should have —

PAUL: Wo wo wo — slow down.

STEPHEN: I met with Tom Duffy last night.

PAUL: You *what*?

STEPHEN: He called me just after you left for the airport and asked to meet. I asked what it was about, and he said it was really important. So I did. I met with him. Shit, I shoud've called / you. I —

PAUL: Stop. Let me get this straight. You met with Tom Duffy?

STEPHEN: Yes.

PAUL: What'd he want?

STEPHEN: Well first he — look — the gist of it is he wants to hire me. He wants me to jump ship and come work for him. This is bad, Paul. He showed me poll numbers with Pullman already ahead by four. They've been telling their supporters to pose as Morris people to the pollsters. We're in really deep fucking trouble.

PAUL: That can't be true. He was playing mind games with you.

STEPHEN: He laid out their whole plan. Robo-calls, traffic jams, fake lit, and fucking Thompson. Promised him secretary of labor and told him to lead us on. Everything you told him last night's gonna go straight to Duffy's ear.

PAUL: If this is some sort of practical — I mean — my fucking blood pressure is going through the roof right now.

STEPHEN: I'm sorry, Paul. I really should have called / you.

PAUL: This happened last night?

STEPHEN: Just before the press conference.

PAUL: And you didn't fucking *call* me?

STEPHEN: I'm sorry Paul. I — I don't know. I guess I thought — I thought maybe it wasn't true. Maybe / he was —

PAUL: Jesus Steve. I can't believe you didn't —

STEPHEN: I know I know I know. Look — I was scared. I was scared and totally confused and I thought —

PAUL: It doesn't fucking *matter* what you thought. It matters what you did. It matters what you *didn't* do. If all this shit is true, I made a fucking ass of myself at Thompson's place. And I gave away our whole goddamn strategy. Just handed it over. Do you realize what this — do you have *any* fucking idea?

STEPHEN: I know Paul. Believe me. But it's like — like I was paralyzed. I didn't know if it was even worth telling you about if — if you came back and said — yeah — Thompson's in the bag, but . . . fuck Paul. I don't know.

PAUL: I sure as hell hope you were gonna tell me even if I came back and —

STEPHEN: Of course! Yes. I just —

PAUL: 'Cause I mean, if you were planning on keeping this secret —

STEPHEN: No! Not at all. That's why I'm telling you now.

PAUL: After I tell you Thompson said no.

STEPHEN: Seriously Paul, that's why I'm here now. To tell you. To —

PAUL: A little late now, don't you think? After I —

STEPHEN: You know me Paul. You know I would never — I really should have called last night. I should have and I didn't.

PAUL: You're fucking right you should have. You don't meet secretly with the other guy's campaign manager and *not* fucking tell me about it. You don't get a fucking *call* from the other guy's manager and not tell me.

STEPHEN: This is the *first* time Paul. The first time I've ever really fucked up. And I'm sorry. I am so fucking sorry.

PAUL: It's a pretty big goddamn fuck-up whether it's your first time or not. I mean if we lose here, if we *lose* — then we're *both* out of a job.

STEPHEN: We can figure this out. There has to be a way to figure this out.

PAUL: We *better* figure this the fuck out.

STEPHEN: Paul. Please. You gotta forgive me on this. I feel like absolute shit.

I feel terrible. Last night, I was so — you want to know the truth? I was so wound up about this shit that I went out and got wasted. Totally wasted. Drank myself to oblivion. Slept with some girl I shouldn't have. I dealt with this completely the wrong way. So I'm coming clean now. I came out to the airport to tell you this so we can figure it out. I know if we put our heads together and we — Goddamnit! I'm sorry. I am so so so —

PAUL: Steve.

STEPHEN: I am *so* sorry. I feel like I'm — I feel like —

PAUL: Steve. Stop. It's OK.

STEPHEN: No it isn't.

PAUL: It is. It's OK. You're right. We can figure it out. You did the right thing. You told me, which means that we can do something about it.

STEPHEN: I know there's a way.

PAUL: There's always a way. So take a breath and get yourself together. I need you at your best on this.

STEPHEN: I don't want you to think — I mean — I respect the hell out of you and your respect is something I —

PAUL: You and I are still OK, all right? It's been me and you from the beginning on this thing, and I got a little upset, but that's just because all of this — it's a bit of a shock to me. You're allowed your one fuck-up. So now let's get past that and get to work. Sound good?

STEPHEN: Yeah.

PAUL: Good. Now. First thing we have to do is get to that fucking event in — where is it?

STEPHEN: Cedar Rapids.

PAUL: Cedar Rapids. We got to get to that event in Cedar Rapids so I can break this all to the governor. You can fill me in on the drive out there.

STEPHEN: He's gonna flip.

PAUL: He'll be fine. I know how to handle him. You just do your job and deal with the press.

STEPHEN: I can do that.

PAUL: Of course you can.

STEPHEN: Thanks Paul. Really. I mean —

PAUL: Don't thank me. Just win me this fucking state.

THE GOOD NEGRO
Tracey Scott Wilson

Dramatic
James, thirties
Pelzie, twenties

James is a charismatic civil-rights activist modeled on Martin Luther King Jr. Pelzie's house has been bombed, killing his infant daughter. He blames James for stirring up trouble and does not want him to attend his daughter's funeral.

JAMES: I been thinking about you, praying for you. How are you? How is Claudette?

PELZIE: She ain't good. But better. Little bit

(Pause.)

JAMES: How can I help you? What do you need? Anything. Anything at all.

PELZIE: You ain't speaking at the baby's funeral

JAMES: I respect your wishes. I didn't come for that.

PELZIE: Not you or any of your peoples. We's getting our own man.

JAMES: I understand that. I didn't come to ask you about that. I came to offer myself, my help in any other way, behind the scenes.

PELZIE: I can't stop you from comin' to the funeral but you ain't saying a damn thing.

JAMES: Mr. Sullivan, I am not going to participate. I understand that clearly.

PELZIE: But not 'cause it your fault like 'dette say. I don't believe it your fault or the Movement fault.

JAMES: All right. I appreciate you saying that.

PELZIE: I ain't saying that for you. I come to know some things.

(Pause.)

First, I ain't figure why ya'll was helpin' me and 'dette, then dat Rutherford come round and I see. Ya'll figured 'dette was good for ya'll cause she look nice and talk nice. A good Negro woman for all the peoples. That what ya'll saw. You ain't know her at all. She a good Negro woman, but not 'cause ya'll say so. And now Shelly. She good for ya'll too. 'Cause she just a baby. Can't nobody say 'bout her you ain't talking right or walking right or looking right. 'Cause she just a baby. But ya'll ain't know her either. You ain't know 'dette and you ain't know Shelly. Dat's why you can't speak at the funeral. You hear me Reverend?

JAMES: Yes.

PELZIE: Even the white folks sorry 'bout this. They coming up to me crying. Next week they back to calling me nigger.

JAMES: I am very sorry. I will never be able to express how sorry I am. I didn't want to use anyone. We are all perfect in God's eyes.

PELZIE: Preacher talk.

JAMES: Your daughter's death will not be in vain. This horrible, horrible thing has shown folks how evil segregation is and . . . I . . .

PELZIE: Preacher talk, preacher talk, preacher talk, preacher talk.

(Pause.)

JAMES: *(Continued.)* It will not be in vain.

(Pause.)

JAMES: I wanted to let you know we're going to Florida for a while to work with some students there.

PELZIE: Florida

JAMES: We'll be back in Birmingham but . . . This fight is every where.

PELZIE: You needs to stay here.

JAMES: We won't be gone long. In the meantime, the mayor has promised to appoint a biracial committee.

PELZIE: The mayor? Ain't he the one say I set my house on fire? He gonna do what?

JAMES: We'll see this fight through.

PELZIE: You ain't coming back.

JAMES: No. I will be back.

PELZIE: When? When you coming back?

JAMES: When the time is right.

PELZIE: When dat? You gonna finds you another Shelly another 'dette? Den what?

JAMES: Please. I don't want to . . . I'm going to leave now

(Pelzie blocks James's exit.)

JAMES: I don't want to upset you.

PELZIE: What more upsetting den my dead baby?

JAMES: The whole world is watching. They are waiting for us to fuck it up. They are waiting for us to talk wrong, walk wrong, be wrong, and then they can say see? Look at them niggers. No better than animals. No better. I told you so.

PELZIE: White people don't be talking right or walking right.

JAMES: No, but they got their rights already

PELZIE: So you tell 'em dat. Tell 'em we just like you and we can have the same things you be having. Tell them dat Reverend.

JAMES: It's more complicated than that.

PELZIE: No, it ain't. I knows what you saying and I's still asking you. We's askin' you. I speaking for 'dette now, but that what we's askin' you to do for us. Stays here and fight.

JAMES: I promise you . . .

PELZIE: 'Cause we good enough. We good enough Reverend. You ain't gonna find nobody better than 'dette, better than Shelly. You ain't gonna find nothing that ain't here already so just stay here and fight. Do that for us. For Shelly. Stays here and fight.

LIONS
Vince Melocchi

Dramatic
Spook, thirties
Artie, twenties

We are in a sports bar in Detroit. Spook has recently lost his job. Artie has been gone a while but comes back. He has a job.

ARTIE: . . . says, "Artie, I really appreciate this. Really." An' I say, "Appreciation don't put nothin' in my front pocket. Let's see some scratch."

SPOOK: No shit!

ARTIE: Fuck 'em. Everything got a price, Johnny

SPOOK: Guess.

ARTIE: Yeah. Fuck, yeah. *(Beat.)* How you doin'?

SPOOK: Good. Real good.

ARTIE: Nice. Know, I haven't seen you in what? Four, five years.

SPOOK: Since seventy-six, so six years.

ARTIE: Six years? Wow. But, it's like I talked to you yesterday. You don't change. *(Off his reaction.)* I mean that in a good way.

SPOOK: Thanks.

ARTIE: Know who did change? Lori Palm.

SPOOK: Where'd you —

ARTIE: — happened to her? She looks —

SPOOK: Drinks too much. All she does is drink an' collect welfare checks.

ARTIE: Ooohhh . . .

SPOOK: I look at her, I think, "Get a job, already." How tough can it be?

ARTIE: Nice. *(Beat.)* So what's this "Spook" shit?

SPOOK: Guys over Elias started callin' me Spook 'cause I'd always disappear on certain jobs . . . so, Spook . . . like Casper the ghost an' shit.

ARTIE: I'll stick with Johnny.

SPOOK: Call me asshole, just get your point across.

ARTIE: Asshole.

SPOOK: There ya go!

(They share a laugh.)

SPOOK: . . . two, side. *(Misses.)* Fuck me in the ass.

ARTIE: How are things at the screw factory?

SPOOK: Elias is great! Just got promoted. Was workin' the press, but now I oversee them an' at.

ARTIE: Wearin' a tie?

SPOOK: No, fuck that. I ain't no suit. *(Beat.)* Nothin' personal.

ARTIE: I get it.

SPOOK: Seventy-five cent an hour raise. Two weeks vacation. Five sick days a year. Weekends, most holidays off. Paid. Twelve bucks an hour. Back in school who'd a thought I'd be makin' that kind a cash?

ARTIE: Nice.

SPOOK: Best thing is . . . I always got a case of beers inna backseat and a bag of pot inna glove.

ARTIE: Important.

SPOOK: Laugh, but it is.

ARTIE: I'm not laughing . . . it is. *(Beat.)* So, what else? Still followin' the Lions?

SPOOK: This is our year, man. Big tailgate party before the game Sunday. Wanna come by?

ARTIE: Thanks, but I'm gone tomorrow.

SPOOK: Fast.

ARTIE: Business. Time is money, and all that shit.

SPOOK: Fuckin' suit.

ARTIE: Blow me, mister twelve bucks an' hour an' paid holidays.

SPOOK: Right. So what exactly you doin' now? Sports management or somethin'?

ARTIE: A-S-M. American Sports Management. Did an internship. A lot of work for little or no pay, but the perks are great. Meet a lot of players. Agents. Like that.

SPOOK: Like?

ARTIE: Like Dor-sett.

SPOOK: Tony Dorsett?

ARTIE: Pronounces it Dor-sett, now.

SPOOK: Huh?

ARTIE: Incredible fuckin' asshole, too.

SPOOK: No!

ARTIE: Yeah.

SPOOK: Fuck me! You met Dorsett?

ARTIE: Used to like the prick.

SPOOK: Sucks. Who else?

ARTIE: Bruce Smith.

SPOOK: No!

ARTIE: Matt Millen.

SPOOK: Matt fuckin' Millen! From the Raiders!

ARTIE: Yeah.

SPOOK: Tell me he's a good guy —

ARTIE: Yeah, he's OK. Know who's really nice? Billy Sims.

SPOOK: Our Billy Sims!?

ARTIE: How many are there?

SPOOK: Yeah, just . . . wow. So fuckin' jealous. Kill to be in your shoes.

ARTIE: Yeah?

SPOOK: Fuck, yeah.

ARTIE: It's a lot of hard work, but yeah . . . the perks are sweet. Long hours, boss is kind of a dick . . .

SPOOK: Still. Billy Sims. Matt Millen.

ARTIE: Problem is, guys don't know shit about sports. Know business . . . but not sports.

SPOOK: Huh.

ARTIE: An' in order to make money. *Real* money. You gotta know sports. Know sports, the money comes rollin' in.

(Artie pulls out a wad of money and peals off a twenty. He notices Spook eyeing the cash.)

ARTIE: Chump change, John. Grab us a couple. You fly, I'll buy.

NEXT FALL
Geoffrey Nauffts

Dramatic
Adam, midforties
Luke, twenties

Adam and Luke have just become lovers. The next morning, at breakfast, Luke prays, which startles Adam, who doesn't understand how a gay guy can also be a committed Christian.

ADAM: What was that?
LUKE: What was what?
ADAM: Where'd you go just then?
LUKE: I was praying.
ADAM: You mean, crystals and chakras? Like a Deepak Chopra kind of thing?
LUKE: Not really.
ADAM: Then, who were you praying to?
LUKE: God.

(The honeymoon just ended. Luke takes a big bite of food: Adam smiles, nervously.)

LUKE: Yum.
ADAM: Is that an everyday occurrence?
LUKE: Pretty much.
ADAM: So, you're what, then . . . You're . . .
LUKE: A Christian.
ADAM: OK.

(Adam tries to proceed with breakfast as usual.)

LUKE: Does that freak you out?
ADAM: Does it freak me out?
LUKE: Yeah.
ADAM: Why would it freak me out?
LUKE: No reason . . . Why? What are you?
ADAM: What am I?
LUKE: Besides a vamper.
ADAM: Nothing . . . I don't know. I didn't really grow up with a religion.

(Luke stabs a tomato and pops it in his mouth.)

LUKE: These tomatoes *are* fierce. I don't care what you say.

ADAM: You're gay though, right?

LUKE: Uh . . . whose earlobes do you think you were nibbling all night?

ADAM: I know, but don't Christians consider that a sin?

LUKE: Uh-huh.

(Luke stabs another tomato and pops it in Adam's mouth.)

ADAM: So, how does that work, then?

LUKE: How does what work?

ADAM: Being gay and . . . you know . . .

LUKE: This is gonna be a problem, isn't it?

ADAM: No . . . I'm . . . I just . . .

LUKE: We're all sinners, Adam. We all struggle with one thing or another. That one just happens to be mine.

ADAM: Do you atone then, is that what you do?

LUKE: You really want to talk about this?

ADAM: Sure.

LUKE: *(Matter-of-fact.)* You accept Christ as the son of God. That he died on the cross for all your sins.

ADAM: That's it?

LUKE: Pretty much.

ADAM: And you'll go to heaven?

LUKE: If you believe. If you truly believe.

ADAM: And you do?

LUKE: Uh-huh. *(A beat.)*

ADAM: Then how come you continue to sin? I mean, and don't get me wrong, that was some amazing sinning we just did, I look forward to more, but you sinned a lot. You sinned more than I did.

LUKE: I was hoping we could sin again after breakfast.

ADAM: You didn't answer my question.

LUKE: It's human nature. We can't escape it. But as long as you've accepted Christ . . .

(Another beat.)

ADAM: Is that why you didn't introduce me to your mom last night?

LUKE: I didn't?

ADAM: Nope.

LUKE: Might have had a little something to do with it.

(Luke starts clearing the table.)

ADAM: So, let me see if I got this right. I'm assuming sin is sin. And if your sin is having sex with men, and my sin is, say, killing men who have sex with men, then as long as I've accepted Christ as my Savior, I'll go to heaven with you?

LUKE: Killing men who have sex with men? You mean, like Jeffrey Dalmer?

ADAM: Yeah . . . Well, no. Because he killed them, then he ate them. Plus, he had sex with them too, so no, not him.

LUKE: Like who then?

ADAM: *(Thinking.)* The guys who killed Matthew Shepard.

(A beat.)

LUKE: Technically, yes.

ADAM: Not only that, but I can continue to kill men who have sex with men, much as you continue to have sex with men, every day for the rest of my life, and still go to heaven?

LUKE: Well . . .

ADAM: It's just a hypothesis.

LUKE: I know it sounds terrible, but . . . yes.

ADAM: Huh.

(Another beat.)

ADAM: So then, if Matthew Shepard hadn't accepted Jesus Christ before he died, he's in hell, and his killers who, say, have, are going to heaven? Is that what you're saying?

(Luke stands there with his arms full.)

LUKE: Can we change the subject?

OUR HOUSE
Theresa Rebeck

Comic
Wes, forties
Stu, forties

Wes is the head of programming for a major television network. Stu is his news director. While discussing a young female reporter whom they plan to make a star by putting her on a reality show, Wes vents about the FCC requirement that TV networks have to broadcast news. It loses money, and nobody watches it anyway. Stu, something of a toady, tries to mollify him.

(Stu and Wes watch from his office.)

WES: You think her hair looks all right? You don't think it's too short do you?

STU: Looks fine to me.

WES: I think it's kind of, I mean I love it, but in the Midwest you know what they're all saying. Lesbian! Lesbian!

STU: So what's the question? Do I think Jennifer looks like a lesbian?

WES: God no, we know she doesn't look like a lesbian. What about her breasts? I mean they're beautiful but a little more cleavage is never a bad thing. Don't they have bras with little pumps on them? We should look into that.

STU: I think she looks great.

WES: No arguments from me on that. She looks great, she is great. Nose might be too perfect That's what they say in the chat rooms. Her nose is too perfect! What can I do? She's perfect. Giving two thousand percent. Nevertheless, the numbers still suck.

STU: The numbers are good, Wes.

WES: Don't tell me the numbers are good, Stu. I can't sell shit on the morning news, excuse me that's not true, I can sell slightly more shit on the morning news than I can on the evening news, but the going price for shit is shit. Christ. Americans like optimism. The news division bleeds money, I'm throwing everything I can at it, Jennifer Ramirez, the hottest anchor on the air, and I still can't pull it out of the red. Maybe if I had her, you know, take her clothes off while she was reading the copy. Just kidding, but you know they did that in Europe and it got people to watch.

STU: I'm sure it did.

WES: I wouldn't do that but it would work.

STU: But you wouldn't do that.

WES: But I might fucking think about it. Christ! The fucking news. It's just a flicking loser, no matter what you do; it needs to be canceled altogether. You can't make it work? Then you cancel it. We are fucking canceling all of it.

STU: You can't cancel the news. Wes.

WES: What did you say? Did you say "can't"?

STU: Wes, come on, it's in our contract wit the FCC.

WES: The fucking FCC. You think I give a shit about the FCC? They're flicking morons

STU: The network's contract with the FCC states clearly —

WES: Do not fucking lecture me about my own flicking network! Do you want to keep working here or not?

STU: My point being, Wes, that the airwaves, the deal we have with the government is that we get the airwaves for free.

WES: Nothing's for free in this country.

STU: Well, precisely. That's the deal. They give us the airwaves, we are required by law to present a certain number of hours a week, of news coverage.

WES: Well, then they should pay for it. Has anyone looked into this? The news division loses money hand over fist. You know why? Because nobody gives a shit about the news.

STU: I don't agree with you.

WES: You don't what?

STU: People care, people . . . want to know . . . the world . . . we don't want to to be alone. We want to know . . . our neighbors.

WES: You're fired.

STU: God, Wes, no. I am not disagreeing with you, I see the force of your argument —

WES: You're fired!

STU: *(Suddenly forceful.)* But whether or not you're right doesn't matter! The fact is, we get the airwaves for free. In exchange for that, we have to provide news. Period. End of story. It's the law.

You cannot — you CANNOT cancel the news.

And you can't, God, for that matter you can't dumb it down anymore, you've dumbed it down so far what's left of it mostly resembles a catfood commercial.

WES: Hey I do what I'm forced to do. People like cats.

STU: PEOPLE NEED THE NEWS. And it is our social responsibility.

WES: Our WHAT?

STU: YES, no, no, yes we have a responsibility, it is a holy trust, you can't possibly think — God, I'm here every day performing this soul-sucking sysphian defense of the notion that people deserve the news whether they want it or not because I believe in KNOWLEDGE and INFORMATION because that makes us different and better, yes, better than the lower primates or our our our pets! People need news. If we choose — if we only pump commercials and and and SHIT into their homes through the powerful and and completely unknowable instrument, the TELEVISION SET, if all we do is send out — SHIT — then then we are the ones. We are culpable. Of the destruction of the human race I believe that I really believe that.

WES: So what you're saying is that the human race would be more important to you than the numbers.

STU: What I'm saying is if you try and cancel the news they'll turn on your girlfriend.

WES: Watch yourself.

STU: *(Ignoring the warning.)* They're always looking, you know this, they're always looking for an excuse to turn. If you try to fly in the face of the rules on something this big? She's the one they'll go after. They'll go after both of you together. Wes put too much faith in Jennifer Ramirez.

WES: Fuck you.

STU: They do, actually.

WES: They do?

(Both are silent for a moment. Stu cautiously continues.)

STU: Yes. And CNN —

WES: I got it, Stu; I got it.

(There is another pause.)

STU: I'll go clear out my desk.

WES: What? Why?

STU: You fired me.

WES: Oh for fuck's sake, you're not fired. Somebody's got to run that loser news division. Lose any more money and you ARE fired. No. No. Say anything shitty about Jen? Ever again? Ever? And you're so fucking fired you will never work anywhere again. I will see to it that no one on earth will hire you to clean their toilets, that's how flicking fired you will be.

STU: Understood.

WES: Good.

PARASITE DRAG

Mark Roberts

More information on this playwright may be found in the "Meet Our Authors" tab at www.smithandkraus.com.

Seriocomic
Ronnie Brown, midthirties to forties
Gene Brown, midthirties to forties

Estranged brothers Ronnie and Gene have just lost their drug-addicted sister to AIDS. While discussing her funeral arrangements, painful childhood memories rise to the surface, each man having a different rememberance of the truth.

(Lights up. Gene is sitting on the couch looking at the photo albums. His black eye is more pronounced, and there's no makeup covering it. Ronnie is standing at the front door, looking out. The lighting has a greenish tint to it. We hear the wind outside.)

RONNIE: They say it was a watch or a warning? *(Silence.) Gene?*

GENE: What?

RONNIE: Watch or a warning?

GENE: Warning. *(Pause.)*

RONNIE: Remind me which one's worse.

GENE: "Watch" means the conditions are right. "Warning" means that one has actually been spotted.

RONNIE: So, "warning" is worse?

GENE: Yes.

RONNIE: And they're out driving around in it. Great. *(Ronnie crosses to the kitchen.)* When they coming back?

GENE: She didn't say.

RONNIE: She's your wife. Don't you keep any kind of tabs on her at all?

GENE: I trust her.

RONNIE: Well, that makes you a fucking idiot.

GENE: What's that supposed to mean?

RONNIE: Nothing. Just an expression, Gene. Like "beer-battered."

GENE: Joellen will call me on her cell if there's a problem.

RONNIE: Oh, Mister Big Shot has a cell phone. Kiss my fucking ass.

GENE: Everybody has a cell phone, Ronnie.

RONNIE: Won't catch me owning one of them fucking things. Yacking away behind the wheel of the car. In line at the bank. "I'm so important I have to talk to you right fuckin' now." Kiss my hairy white ass.

GENE: They're good to have in an emergency.

RONNIE: World did just fine without them for many years.

GENE: What if someone needs to get a hold of you in a hurry?

RONNIE: They can wait until I'm somewhere where there's a real phone. Or if I don't want to be found, they can wait until I surface. That way, I'm still holding on to some fucking cards. I'm still doing what I want and not tethered to some kind of tracking device.

GENE: They're not tracking devices.

RONNIE: Don't kid yourself. *(Pause.)*

GENE: Well, they'll be back as soon as they get some clothes for Nadine.

RONNIE: What are you putting her in?

GENE: A dress of some sort.

RONNIE: She never wore a fuckin' dress in her whole life.

GENE: Well, a dress is what she'll be buried in.

RONNIE: At least put her in something people will recognize her in!

GENE: Eighty pounds, rotted teeth, and skin like parchment paper. Doesn't matter what we dress her in. Nobody is going to recognize her.

RONNIE: A dress is not what she would have wanted.

GENE: How do you know what she would have wanted?

RONNIE: *(Screaming.)* You remember how she'd throw a fit every time Mom would try to get a dress on her!

(Gene, furious, throws the photo album at Ronnie.)

RONNIE: Jesus!

GENE: I don't give a shit! Put her in a pair of filthy jeans if you want. Will that do the trick for you? How about a belt wrapped around her arm? That should get the point across. Here we go. Maybe we could get some fuckin' . . . nigger to piss on her in the casket! *(Breaking.)* That work? *(Pause. Distant thunder outside. Ronnie carefully picks up the photo album, crosses to the dining room table, and sits.)*

RONNIE: Dress her however you want.

GENE: Thank you. *(Long pause. Ronnie thumbs through the photo album.)*

RONNIE: Remember that black-and-white checked one, the one just like Mom's?

(Gene nods.)

GENE: Yeah. There's home movies of it somewhere.

RONNIE: Two of them looked like twins. *(Beat.)* What were we all dressed up for that day, anyway?

GENE: Easter Sunday.

RONNIE: That's right. It was Easter. *(Beat.)* Smell of that egg dye.

GENE: Yeah. We were still in the house on Vorcey.

RONNIE: I drove by it today.

(Pause. Gene looks at him, stands, and crosses to the kitchen.)

GENE: Ronnie, I'd like you to be one of Nadine's pallbearers.

RONNIE: I don't think so.

GENE: Be a big help.

RONNIE: Pass.

GENE: I need you.

RONNIE: I'm not doin' it.

GENE: Are you kidding me?

RONNIE: No. I'm not kidding you. Quit asking me.

GENE: One simple favor. Unbelievable.

RONNIE: I'm not even gonna be here.

GENE: Not gonna be where?

RONNIE: Leaving town as soon as Susie gets back.

GENE: You're kidding me. You're not staying for her funeral?

RONNIE: No. I'm not.

GENE: Why?

RONNIE: I don't need to see Nadine like that.

GENE: See her like what? Dead? You have to see her like that —

RONNIE: That thing is not my sister. I don't know what that is.

GENE: That is our sister, Ronnie. And you wanna know something? I've seen her look a lot worse.

RONNIE: Well, then you deal with this. 'Cause . . . I can't.

GENE: Don't make me walk through this by myself.

RONNIE: You're not by yourself. Joellen will be with you. *(Standing.)* Where the fuck are they, anyway? *(Ronnie crosses to the front door.)*

GENE: Ronnie, look. I just . . . whatever has gone on between us doesn't matter. It's important that we have some closure with her.

RONNIE: I don't know what that means. But . . . you'll just have to struggle through it.

GENE: I'm asking you for this one favor. And then you'll never have to lay eyes on me again.

RONNIE: Can't help you. *(Pause.)*

GENE: Mom and Dad would want us to do this together.

RONNIE: *(Smiling.)* You're gonna play the family card? Jesus, Gene. I'll kick in a few dollars on expenses and everything, but don't turn this into a Hallmark fucking moment.

GENE: You're not really this hard of a person. I know it. You can't be.

RONNIE: Brother, you don't know shit. What you're seeing right now is my chewy center.

GENE: No matter what went on, we started out as a family.

RONNIE: Well, dog shit starts out as a Kibble. But, I ain't eatin' either one. *(Gene crosses to him.)*

GENE: I want to make amends with you. I want us to heal the wounds that we have inflicted on one another. You've hurt me, and I know that I've hurt you.

RONNIE: Is this when Oprah comes out and we hug and cry?

GENE: Ronnie, I have found a faith in God that gets me through times like these. And I think you could benefit greatly.

RONNIE: Gene, if you're tryin' to get me to board the Jesus bus, you're wasting your fucking gas.

GENE: Joellen was right. We're the only ones left to prove we ever were a family.

RONNIE: Tell you what, Gene, if you die before me, I'll make sure you're buried in something snazzy. And I trust you'll do the same for —

GENE: Ronnie, please don't do this. Please don't walk out on this. You weren't here when Dad died —

RONNIE: I was too busy dancin' in the fuckin' streets.

GENE: He loved you, Ronnie.

(Ronnie moves toward Gene, threateningly.)

RONNIE: That dead-eyed, drunk, hateful, piece of shit didn't love —

GENE: Don't call him names.

RONNIE: . . . Anybody. And I hope he's getting fucked in hell . . .

GENE: Don't say that.

RONNIE: . . . with a red-hot poker.

GENE: He loved you.

RONNIE: Goody.

GENE: He raised a family. Fed and clothed his children.

RONNIE: Yeah, everything was hunky-dory, Gene.

GENE: He worked two jobs to make sure his children never went hungry.

RONNIE: That lets him off the hook for all the other? 'Cause we were fed?

GENE: Left home when he was fourteen years old, no education, managed to make something of his life.

RONNIE: Why you pinning medals on that piece of shit?

GENE: He's my father.

RONNIE: He was Nadine's father too.

GENE: He was an uneducated man.

RONNIE: Don't take an education, Gene.

GENE: He grew up poor, ignorant, and didn't know any better.

RONNIE: Didn't know any better than to fuck his own daughter? *(Beat.)* Even dogs know not to do that, Gene! *(Beat.)* Jesus Christ. Let's call a spade a spade. Not pretend we had Robert-fucking-Young sleeping down the hall. *(Long pause. Ronnie crosses to the front door.)*

GENE: Lost himself when Mom died. *(Gene crosses to the table and sits.)*

RONNIE: Found himself in Nadine's bedroom didn't he?

GENE: You don't know what was going on in there.

RONNIE: You're right, Gene. I can only assume. I don't have any real hard evidence. Maybe the fact that he'd wait until we were in bed to go in there was a tip-off. Turn on her record player, so we couldn't hear the whispering and the crying. "Oh very young, what will you leave us this time?" What happens to your guts when you hear that song, Gene? I've actually had to pull over before to puke.

GENE: Mom was the love of his life. He was devastated.

RONNIE: Certainly honored her memory, didn't he? Raping her only daughter —

GENE: Don't say things like that. It's ugly.

RONNIE: Never wondered why he got up so early to do the laundry every Saturday? Didn't want us seeing her bloody bedsheets.

GENE: Don't.

RONNIE: That's fucking ugly.

GENE: Stop.

RONNIE: Split her wide open.

GENE: He loved her.

RONNIE: A little too much, you ask me.

GENE: She was always climbing on him and kissing on him.

RONNIE: The bitch was asking for it.

GENE: He fell apart when Mom killed herself.

RONNIE: Had nothing to do with Mom killing herself.

GENE: He was lonely and sad. He went off the tracks.

RONNIE: He was sneaking down the hall long before Mom died.

GENE: That's not true.

RONNIE: Where did you grow up, Gene? At the home across the street? That shit went on for at least a year before Mom took the top of her head off.

GENE: They did the best they could with what they had. They made mistakes, everybody does. But, they wanted good for all of their children, and they tried to raise us in a good Christian home.

RONNIE: I don't know who the fuck you are. I truly don't. I mean, you've always been a flighty little shit, but this is fantasyland.

(Gene crosses to Ronnie.)

GENE: Remember Mom used to hide Three Musketeers bars in our hooded sweatshirts?

RONNIE: What the fuck are you talking about?

GENE: Remember going to Lake of the Woods . . . ?

RONNIE: I remember Mom sitting in her car for eight solid hours . . .

GENE: Getting a Superman costume for Christmas . . .

RONNIE: . . . When I left for school, and there when I got home.

GENE: Two weeks vacation.

RONNIE: Cigarette after cigarette.

GENE: Layin' on the floor in front of that old Zenith.

RONNIE: Belt marks across my legs.

GENE: "Ladies and gentlemen, the star of our show . . ."

RONNIE: Nadine hiding in the garage . . .

GENE: "Mister Jackie Gleason." *(À la Gleason.)* "And away we go."

(Ronnie slaps Gene.)

RONNIE: Put that shit away!

(Gene crosses to the table and sits. He begins to weep. Long pause. Ronnie crosses to him, slowly.)

RONNIE: You want a memory? I remember walking in on Mom in the bathroom. She was taking a steak knife to her legs. Cutting little hunks out of her flesh and flickin' them at the wall. Blood all over the bathmat. Tiny pieces of skin and meat stuck to the tile. Her eyes wild. I stood there holding my breath, watching my mother mutilate herself. It took her a good five minutes to realize I was even in the room. And she just looked right through me. Her expression didn't change. She just kept right on digging pieces out of herself. *(Pause.)*

GENE: You left me there to fend for myself. *(Ronnie crosses to the front door.)*

RONNIE: Had to go, Gene.

GENE: Why didn't you take me with you? That day, that day you left?

RONNIE: Had to be on my own, Gene.

GENE: I ran after you. He screamed at me.

RONNIE: Had to get as far away as I could.

GENE: You left.

RONNIE: Not before I opened his head with an ashtray, I didn't. Not before I threw him out of the house and beat the shit out of him. Not before I ran up and down the street screaming, "My dad fucks my sister." After that, I left. And I believe after that Nadine was able to get a few hours sleep at night.

GENE: You left me there with him.

RONNIE: *(Screaming violently.)* I know I did, Gene!

GENE: You were my brother. *(Pause.)*

RONNIE: I couldn't look at you any more. I thought to call you a hundred times over the years. But, I just didn't want to hear your voice.

GENE: Why?

RONNIE: Your voice is my voice. And it carries too much shame.

(Pause. Ronnie sits on the couch.)

GENE: I fall to my knees every night, praying to God to lighten my heart. To bring me some kind of peace. It doesn't come. I just get up off of my knees and lay down next to a woman that doesn't love me. And I have no feelings for her whatsoever. I don't feel anything. Pleasure, excitement. It's not part of my world. I just get up and walk through every day, waiting for something to happen. Waiting for God to show me some kind of sign.

RONNIE: Gene, there is no God. And if there is, He's using you for a fucking punching bag.

GENE: I can't believe that's true. I can't believe there's nobody watching out for us.

RONNIE: Gene. There's nobody watching out for us. No God, no government, and if you had a brain in your head, you'd toss that cellular phone out the window. You're kidding yourself if you think that shit ain't monitored.

GENE: Ronnie, this can't be it. There has to be someone who loves us, who watches out for us.

RONNIE: Let go of it, brother.

GENE: It was God's mercy that ended Nadine's suffering.

RONNIE: I didn't see Him when I was at the hospital. I didn't see any God in sight. Or a doctor, or a nurse, or a fucking janitor for that matter. I just saw our sister staring into space. Wincing every once in a while from the pain. That's all I saw. No God on the premises.

(Gene crosses to Ronnie and gets down on one knee, next to him.)

GENE: Ronnie, pray with me. Humble yourself in front of Him.

RONNIE: Her face looked the way it did that day I broke down her door.

GENE: *(Praying.)* Heavenly Father, we come to You today on bended knees . . .

RONNIE: Scared. Helpless.

GENE: . . . and we ask You to pray for the soul of our dear sister . . .

RONNIE: Son of a bitch layin' on top of her . . .

GENE: . . . as she passes from this world, to a life eternal with You. Dear Lord . . .

RONNIE: Glass ashtray slowed him down pretty good.

GENE: And pray for my brother tonight as he struggles with his own faith. Put him on a path, dear Lord . . . *(Gene continues to quietly pray.)*

RONNIE: My path was clear, Gene. Couldn't let her lay there suffering. Couldn't let her last moments on this earth be more painful than her whole life was. I just couldn't allow that. I mean, maybe there is a God, Gene. I sure felt some kind of divine power working through me. And I didn't even think for a second about it being wrong. I just put the pillow over her face, Gene.

GENE: Dear Lord, watch over all of us . . .

(Ronnie takes Gene's head and whispers in his ear.)

RONNIE: *(Through tears.)* Didn't take much to hold her down. Not enough strength in her to put up a fight. It was over in about forty seconds. Couple of little kicks and that was it. Pulled the pillow off, closed her eyes, and it was done. And I don't feel any regrets, Gene. I don't feel any remorse. What I did was a good thing. Ended her suffering. I didn't add to it. No matter what you think, I stopped it. Stopped it twice. Once when she was a girl and once last night. So, don't ever tell me I never did anything for our sister, Gene. I loved her. I did my part.

(Gene opens his eyes.)

GENE: Don't leave me again. Don't leave me with all of this.

RONNIE: I can't help you, Gene. It kills me to look at you.

(Ronnie breaks away and crosses to the front door.)

GENE: You're my brother, let me come with you.

RONNIE: I gotta travel light, Gene. My wings can't take the extra weight. There's a name for it. Can't remember what it is. Aeronautical term.

GENE: I got nothing here. I got no life. *(Crying.)* Don't leave me behind.

(Ronnie crosses to the table.)

RONNIE: It's the parts of an airplane that don't contribute to flight. Fuselage, landing gear . . . and what the hell is that called?

GENE: You're my brother. We slept in the same room. We had the same life. We're the same.

RONNIE: Parasite drag. *(Gene goes to Ronnie and tries to hold him. Ronnie shakes him off.)* Get off of me. I can't carry you. I cannot carry you.

ROCKET CITY, ALABAM'

Mark Saltzman

More information on this playwright may be found in the "Meet Our Authors" tab at www.smithandkraus.com.

Dramatic
Amy Lubin, twenty-one
U.S. Army Major Hamilton Pike Jr., thirty-two

The Cold War has begun, and America must compete with the Soviet Union in creating the most powerful weapons of the era: guided missiles with atomic warheads. The American missile program is headed up by U.S. Army Major Hamilton Pike Jr., an all-American, Princeton-educated rich boy with political ambitions who has quietly slipped Hitler's top rocket scientists into the country and settled them in Huntsville, Alabama, where the missiles are to be built. Amy Lubin, an outspoken Jewish girl from New York who is engaged to an Alabama boy, learns about the past of the Germans living in her new hometown and creates a public protest.

MAJOR PIKE: "To investigate and expose the crimes of these Nazis." Your writing has gotten more forceful. I thought I explained the situation with these men.

AMY: You lied. You said they "decided to work for us."

MAJOR PIKE: They did.

AMY: They surrendered to us when the war was lost. They jumped from the sinking ship. The instinct of rats.
(A beat.)

MAJOR PIKE: You've been busy. Printing these fliers, leafletting at the arsenal gates.

AMY: Am I doing anything illegal?

MAJOR PIKE: It's a free country. As long as we keep the Russians at bay. And all the while — as I read in Mrs. Pruitt's column — you're planning your wedding. Limitless energies. You're a rocket engine yourself.

AMY: American design.

MAJOR PIKE: Does your husband-to-be approve what you're doing? Or doesn't he know about this?

AMY: Jed? *(Slightly arch.)* Oh, you know he's considering that job offer.

MAJOR PIKE: Yes, he said he'd check with his fiancee. Good fella, that Jed. Knows his way around the sky. Knows the people and the countryside here. *(Slight threat.)* He'll rise high in the program if no one messes it up for him.

AMY: *(Cold, distant.)* We're discussing the offer. You can understand that it's a private matter between us.

MAJOR PIKE: Good fella, that Jed. But this *(Holding up the leaflet.)* is a public embarrassment that I can not have. People are asking questions, writing letters. I've worked my charm to the limit changing the attitude around here, and you're pushing back my clock. I made a promise to the president. To deliver him an American missile system to keep our nation secure.

AMY: Bringing ex-Nazis into the deepest workings of our most important weapons? That will keep the nation secure?

MAJOR PIKE: Did they not choose our country when they surrendered?

AMY: As opposed to surrendering to who? The Russians? England? I can imagine many things the British would have done with Von Braun — giving him television time with Mickey Mouse isn't one.

MAJOR PIKE: *(With a smile.)* Oh you watched. He did well I thought.

AMY: Very well.

MAJOR PIKE: Television. It's another new science. Exciting, all the ways it can be used.

AMY: Selling detergent and whitewashing Nazis.

MAJOR PIKE: Nuremberg is over. The judges have all gone home.

AMY: There's a courthouse right in the middle of town. Perfect for a trial.

MAJOR PIKE: You'd have no case.

AMY: They were members of the Nazi party.

(The Major fires his shot.)

MAJOR PIKE: But about to become American citizens.

(Amy is stopped cold by that information.)

AMY: No, you can't! You can't give them citizenship!

MAJOR PIKE: Can and will. I have friends high up at the State Department who helped push it through.

AMY: Making Nazis American citizens!

MAJOR PIKE: German scientists who were forced to work for the Reich. These men were not fanatical Nazis.

AMY: Oh, not fanatical! They were building weapons to help Hitler conquer the world, and their hearts weren't into it, the poor things? How awful it must have been, watching London in flames and feeling a little uncomfortable about it. "Not fanatical" — Von Braun was a major in the SS. He created a factory, underground. Slave labor, Jewish prisoners, working them to their deaths in darkness and filth to build those damn rockets of his.

MAJOR PIKE: How did you — ? Oh, your brother's friends in Navy intelligence. *(A beat.)* You know, they found a Japanese soldier last month on an island in Indonesia. Did you hear about it? He fired on his rescuers. He didn't believe the war was over.

AMY: Yes, and?

MAJOR PIKE: I'd say he's like you. The war is over and another is beginning. No gunshots yet, just preparation. The Russians are preparing. They're building missiles. I figure their missiles, like the ones we're making, can travel about two or three hundred miles before going down. Their next ones — three or four hundred miles. We're going to have to keep up. I want us to have a missile that will reach Moscow before the Russians build one that will reach Washington. Or the Bronx. And do you know who they have designing their missiles?

AMY: I can't guess.

MAJOR PIKE: German rocketeers who worked for Hitler. Yes, the Russians also captured a few. But I'll tell you what they don't have: Wernher Von Braun. And they also don't have objections from their people. No one would dare speak out the way you do. And I'm determined to preserve that right in our country. So we'll have our missiles ready to shoot down their missiles over the Atlantic. We'll have our missiles ready in submarines, in underground silos all over the country. Every one of our cities protected by hidden missiles. Every one of our cities, a Rocket City.

AMY: That's insanity.

MAJOR PIKE: Maybe. But it's the future of warfare and international politics.

AMY: People won't let this happen.

MAJOR PIKE: If there's anything the last war taught us, Amy, people will let anything happen. World politics will be determined by what country has atomic warhead missiles and what country doesn't And that's how it will be until we invent something better. Or worse.

AMY: But why should Von Braun and the rest of them live here in luxury while other Nazis are in prison?

MAJOR PIKE: Oh Amy, you know the answer: Because we need them. They can do more for us in Huntsville than they could in a Nuremberg jail.

AMY: But it's wrong. It's morally wrong.

MAJOR PIKE: No, it's morally questionable. That's nothing we'd ever say to the general public, but I'll say that to you. Sometimes, unfortunately, such things must be done. You see things in black and white, don't you Amy? Like the movies.

AMY: Maybe I do.

MAJOR PIKE: I know a little bit about the movies. And they aren't really black and white at all. They're really darker and lighter shades of gray. During the war, it did seem like a black-and-white world. And now — it's like a movie. A world of grays.

AMY: Not to me.

MAJOR PIKE: It's the postwar reality, Amy.

AMY: Then I'm not made for it. I still have to answer to Daniel in my conscience. Not just Daniel, all those lives lost, in London, in Von Braun's rocket factories. This can't go unpunished.

THE SECRET LIFE OF SEAGULLS

Henry Meyerson

More information on this playwright may be found in the "Meet Our Authors" tab at www.smithandkraus.com.

Seriocomic
Don, midthirties
Jim, midthirties

Old friends Don and Jim would rather talk golf than discuss their screwed-up marriages.

(Jim and Don are sitting at a table in a coffee shop.)

JIM: You remember the eighth hole on that course.
DON: Dog leg left?
JIM: Right.
DON: I think it's left, Jimmy.
JIM: No, I mean you're right, it's left.
DON: Got ya.
JIM: What, about 310 to the pin, right?
DON: Yeah.
JIM: Reached it with a driver and wedge.
DON: Get out.
JIM: Dropped it pin high.
DON: Get out.
JIM: Knocked it down for a birdy wordy, Donny, baby.
DON: Son of a gun.
JIM: Even better. On the twelfth . . .
DON: About 515?
JIM: Exactly.
DON: Sand traps.
JIM: Like the fucking Sahara.
DON: So?
JIM: Driver, three wood, nine iron, one putt and gone, baby.
DON: You birdied the twelfth?
JIM: You got it.
DON: Get out.

JIM: Birdy wordy, Donny, baby.

DON: Good going, big guy.

JIM: Yup. Two birdy wordies for the round.

DON: What'd you shoot for the round?

JIM: The whole round?

DON: Yeah. With the two birdies, what'd you shoot?

JIM: 104.

DON: That's not a score, Jimmy, it's a fever.

JIM: Sure, Don, never mind my good holes. You always have to be a downer. I tell you my good stuff, you make sure to bring up my bad.

DON: Just asking.

JIM: Well, sometimes you should lighten up, Donny.

DON: I feel light. Sometimes you ignore the dark side, Luke.

JIM: Very funny.

DON: Just trying to "lighten up."

JIM: You play in Florida?

DON: Yeah.

JIM: How'd you make out, Tiger?

DON: Fine.

JIM: Liar.

DON: Just fine, thank you.

JIM: You're not going to tell, are you?

DON: Not after this little exchange. I'd be like a sitting duck.

JIM: Annie go with you?

DON: Of course.

JIM: She play.

DON: Yup.

JIM: This is like pulling teeth.

DON: You ask, I tell.

JIM: How is Annie?

DON: She tends to slice and not much of a short game.

JIM: How is Annie?

DON: I left her.

JIM: Where?

DON: At the beach.

JIM: Don't blame you. I hate the beach.

DON: I left her.

JIM: Yeah, you said. That's how come you're here.

DON: I mean I left her.

JIM: Left as in left left.

DON: As in bye-bye.

JIM: At the beach.

DON: Staring into the sea and babbling about seagulls shitting on people. After five days of listening to her, I felt staples were being driven into my head.

JIM: You never see that happen, do you?

DON: Of course you don't. The staples thing is just a figure of speech.

JIM: I was talking about the seagulls. Given the number of seagulls at the beach, you'd think you would have seen at least once in a while someone get shat on.

DON: Is that a real word?

JIM: Which?

DON: Shat.

JIM: No idea, but you get the point. Have you heard from her?

DON: Who?

JIM: Anne.

DON: No.

JIM: You haven't spoken?

DON: Not a word.

JIM: You've been married . . .

DON: Ten years.

JIM: And you just . . .

DON: No, not just, Jim. Jeez, give me some credit.

JIM: So how long . . . ?

DON: About a week.

JIM: Still sounds like a . . .

DON: Not a snap decision, Jim. Plenty of thought went into this. *(Beat.)* Well, maybe not plenty, but enough. It was the fucking seagulls put it over the edge.

JIM: Yeah, I can see that.

DON: Where's Sandy?

JIM: Not sure. When I got back a couple of days ago from the golfing thingee, she wasn't here.

DON: Ah. You thought she would be home, then.

JIM: No reason to think otherwise, right? I mean she's always been home when I got there.

DON: Didn't she go with you on this trip?

JIM: Yeah.

DON: So . . .

JIM: I was putting out the seventh hole, turned around, and she was gone. When I got back to the room she was gone. I just figured she'd gotten bored and went home.

DON: So what did you do?

JIM: Finished out the weekend. Beautiful course.

DON: Yeah, I remember.

JIM: Two birdy wordies.

DON: She leave a note?

JIM: No.

DON: Well, at least we know she's not with her mother.

JIM: How do we know that?

DON: Isn't her mother dead?

JIM: Oh, that's right. Boy, that old lady hated me.

DON: Why's that?

JIM: She thought I played too much golf. Apparently her ex-husband played a lot of golf.

DON: That would be Sandy's . . .

JIM: No. That was her stepfather. Her father just disappeared one day.

DON: How do you disappear?

JIM: Way Sandy tells it, he left the house to buy some cough drops and never came home.

DON: So there was no note?

JIM: From her father?

DON: No, Sandy.

JIM: Nope.

DON: Anything missing?

JIM: Some of her clothes.

SLIPPING
Daniel Talbott

Dramatic
Eli, fifteen
Chris, seventeen

Alone, numb, and friendless after the violent death of his father, high school senior Eli moves with his mom from San Francisco to a fresh start in Iowa. A new relationship with a boy named Jake at school exposes Eli again to the possibility of closeness and the danger of being swallowed by it. In this scene, Eli and high school senior Chris sit on a beach at the Marin Headlands, California, immediately after Eli's father's funeral. Both attempt to reach out to each other — the openly bisexual Eli and the severely conflicted and closeted Chris — and the harder they try the more the walls close in on their passionate and abusive relationship. (Note: The use of " . . . . " constitutes a beat, a breath, a change in thought, a shift, maybe a thought within a thought.)

(The beach. 1 a.m. Eli's in a suit jacket and Chris has a black sweater and jacket. Long silence. The sound of waves. Sounds of the ocean.)

CHRIS: It's really late.

ELI: . . . .

CHRIS: I need to get going.
My parents'll be pissed if I'm not home.

ELI: . . . .

(Silence. The ocean.)

CHRIS: It seemed nice. Like . . .
There were a lot of people there.

ELI: Yeah.

CHRIS: You have a big family.

ELI: . . . .

CHRIS: You close?

ELI: Not really.
It's all my dad's.
My mother was . . .
Wasn't really a big hit with the in-laws.

CHRIS: Yeah.
Family can be funny.
My mother can't stand her sisters.
She thinks they're all a bunch of back-stabbing cunts out to fuck my grandparents.
ELI: Yeah.
CHRIS: I liked the song.
My dad loves it.
He loves that album.
Says it reminds him of growing up.
Reminds him of his brothers.
He used to listen to it as a kid all the time.
ELI: . . . .
CHRIS: It's good.
ELI: Yeah.
(Short silence.)
CHRIS: It was weird meeting your mom.
I didn't really know what to say.
ELI: . . . .
(Silence. The ocean.)
CHRIS: I wish you were a girl.
(Short pause.)
CHRIS: *(Continued.)* Kendra thinks you are.
Like a girl trapped in a guy's body.
(Silence. The ocean.)
ELI: I didn't recognize half the people there today.
I didn't know who they were or what they were talking about.
I kept thinking I was in the wrong place.
Like at the wrong funeral.
It wasn't registering.
I couldn't . . .
People kept saying sorry, but I couldn't make it out.
(Beat.)
I wanted to touch you.
I kept wanting to hold your hand.
I wanted you to sit with me.
(Silence. The ocean.)
CHRIS: My parents don't want us hanging out anymore.
They don't want us seeing each other.

ELI: Why?

CHRIS: They think you're sick.

They think you're fucked up and you're rubbing off on me.

(Short pause.)

ELI: What do you think?

CHRIS: That I can't help it if you like guys.

That you need to figure your shit out.

That I have a girlfriend.

That I don't give a fuck about you.

That if you ever call me or try to touch me again I'll fucking kill you.

That the only reason I'm here is 'cause your pussy-ass father killed himself in a car accident.

(Silence.)

SLOW FALLING BIRD
Christine Evans

More information on this playwright may be found in the "Meet Our Authors" tab at www.smithandkraus.com.

Dramatic
Rick, midthirties
Micko, late twenties to early thirties

Slow Falling Bird *is set in the early 2000s at Woomera Immigration Detention Centre. It's a hot, remote hell-hole in the South Australian desert where Middle Eastern asylum seekers are mandatorily detained, due to a "get tough on immigration" policy. Once a U.S. army base and satellite spy center, the town has been revitalized by the private prison industry and the sudden influx of detained refugees. In this play, Woomera is at once a real place and a hallucination within a kind of desert of the mind. Rick and Micko are prison guards. Rick is an old-timer with a short fuse and problems at home; Micko is the new guy, a bit younger than Rick. He's a bit adrift, playing down his part-Aboriginal background and anxious to fit in. We first meet them in this scene on lookout, guarding the long, vacant, perimeter fence in the midday sun. (Note: A backslash [/] indicates where the next line of dialogue overlaps the current one.)*

(Micko and Rick are on lookout. They squint out toward the perimeter fence.)

MICKO: *(Spotting movement.)* What was that?
RICK: Where?
MICKO: There! You see? Right by the fence!
RICK: Nup.
(They stare for a while.)
MICKO: There it goes.
RICK: Rabbit.
(Beat.)
MICKO: The worst thing about this dump is the heat.
RICK: It's not the heat mate.
MICKO: Heat's pretty bad.

RICK: Yup. *(Beat.)* It's hot all right. *(Beat.)* Nah, the worst thing is that it doesn't let up.

MICKO: 'S what I said.

RICK: Nope, it's different. The worst thing's the boredom.

MICKO: Yeah, not much to do.

RICK: Four head counts a day, talk about useless. Same heads, nothing in 'em except misery and lice.

(Beat.)

MICKO: Mate. You ever think about leaving?

RICK: Nope.

MICKO: Big world out there. Not that you can see much of it from here.

RICK: You see enough. Way to the pub. Way home. My wife's pretty face. What else do you need?

MICKO: Something different.

RICK: Like what?

MICKO: I dunno. Something old, like in Europe.

RICK: It's different for blow-ins like you. I grew up here when the Yanks were doing all the early warning missile stuff. Top secret, special access only — place was crawling with spies and special services. Pub was like a beer fountain. Always something going on, F1-11s flying in the top blokes for meetings, you felt like you were part of / something, you know?

MICKO: *(Spotting movement.)* What was that?

RICK: Where?

MICKO: Over there. *(They squint out.)* It's gone now.

RICK: What is this, the bunny-rabbit police?

MICKO: Sorry.

RICK: Relax. *(Beat.)* Eyes play tricks on you, it's the sun.

MICKO: Bright, all right.

RICK: Fucking blinding.

MICKO: And nothing for miles. Flat as a day-old beer.

RICK: Old lady's tit.

MICKO: Snake on the Hume Highway.

RICK: Fart joke at a funeral.

(Beat.)

MICKO: Yep, she's flat, all right.

RICK: Should have seen it when the Yanks were here, everything shined up. Seven thousand here, everyone working — man, once they left we couldn't scrape up a footy team. My first job after the Yanks closed down the army base was painting the playgrounds. Just painting a bunch of the old missiles they left behind for the kids. Blue, like Thomas the Tank Engine. They looked pretty good in the red dirt. But it was fucking depressing, working all day on a playground with no kids in it.

MICKO: Must have been real quiet. I like the quiet out here. You can hear yourself stop thinking.

RICK: You're full of bullshit mate. Quiet means dead. The camp rescued this town from the morgue.

MICKO: Yeah well, the money's good. But you'd want it to be.

RICK: What do you mean?

MICKO: Oh, you know. The kids. Cutting themselves up and all that. That's stressful, that is.

RICK: That stuff just goes straight through me. It's like the heat, it's always there. Sends you to sleep. *(Beat.)* Wouldn't mind waking up occasionally.

MICKO: Yeah well, you get pretty lively down at Spud's.
(Sings, parodying Rick.) — Do you remember when —
We used to sing. Sha na na na / na na na.

RICK: Come on, that's only when we're shitfaced.

MICKO: When *you're* shitfaced, you mean.

RICK: What do you do for fun? Go home and beat off to porn movies?
(Beat.)

MICKO: You were just saying how great it was here

RICK: Bullshit. I said I grew up here.
(Beat.)

MICKO: How's Joy?

RICK: The same. Beautiful.

MICKO: You should think about getting out.

RICK: She doesn't like going out.

MICKO: I mean — a trip or something.

RICK: She likes being at home. She's a homemaker.

MICKO: Well, yeah / but —

RICK: Wouldn't mind something real happening, know what I mean?

MICKO: Like what? Another riot? Camp to burn down?

RICK: Nah, stuff inside doesn't count. Something real. Something that would wake me up. Know what I mean?

MICKO: Yeah. — No, not really.

RICK: Forget it. — *(Beat.)* — What was that? — Over there.
(Micko springs to alert, looking out. Rick laughs at him.)

RICK: Bunny-rabbit alert.

MICKO: *(Amiably.)* You prick.

RICK: Dickhead.
MICKO: Shit-for-brains.
RICK: Wanker.
MICKO: Moron.
RICK: Bunny-fucker.

(Beat. They stand looking out.)

RICK: It's hot, all right.

SMUDGE
Rachel Axler

More information on this playwright may be found in the "Meet Our Authors" tab at www.smithandkraus.com.

Comic
Pete, thirties
Nicholas, thirties

Pete and Nicholas are brothers who work for the census bureau. Nicholas has been acting strangely lately due to the recent birth of his horribly deformed daughter. Pete doesn't know about this yet. All he knows is that his brother has been sending out rather demented census questionnaires, and he wants to know why.

(Nicholas at work. Pete sticks his head over the cubicle wall.)

PETE: Hey, uh, bro. You got a minute.

NICHOLAS: I'm actually in the middle of —

PETE: No, I'm telling you. You've got a minute. Sixty seconds. Go.

(Pause.)

NICHOLAS: . . . Go where?

PETE: "Go" as in "talk." "Go" as in "explain."

(Nicholas just stares at him.)

PETE: No? You need a hint? OK. *(Stretching.)* Ohhh, yawn, yawn, I'm so tired, what?! Is there a pig in here?

NICHOLAS: Sorry?

PETE: I said, is there a pig in here?

NICHOLAS: What are you talking about?

PETE: I dunno, you tell me. We got a couple of calls about the new round of surveys. Apparently, someone snuck in a little supplemental.

Anything you maybe wanted to mention?

Weirdo violent questionnaire, fifty-two, fifty-one . . . Tick-tick, bro. You're wasting my time and yours. And time is money, which is power, which is money, which neither of us is gonna have pretty soon when we both lose our jobs over this which is why you better start talking in the next two seconds.

One second.

NICHOLAS: It wasn't weird.

PETE: Can't hear you.

NICHOLAS: It wasn't weird. Or violent. Just a short survey.

PETE: Man, swear to crap, I wish we were still kids, so I could beat you up. *(He holds up a copy of the survey.)* It *is* weird. It's, like, gnomes-in-a-cuckoo-clock weird. *And* it's violent, *and* it's no-joke, one-hundred-percent, honest-to-fuck *long*.

NICHOLAS: If you've already seen it, why are you asking me about it?

PETE: *(Reading.)* "Would you kill a pig? If yes, continue below. If no, turn to page two." First question! Would you kill a fucking pig?

NICHOLAS: Would you?

PETE: Why would I want to kill a pig? I don't even know what you're talking about.

NICHOLAS: Then turn to page two.

(Beat. Pete does.)

PETE: "Is it OK for a hog farmer to kill a pig?"

"Have you ever eaten bacon?"

"Are you a vegetarian-slash-Kosher?"

"Have you ever been a member or groupie of a hardcore or thrash metal band?"

NICHOLAS: I was being rigorous.

PETE: Oh, here's a good one. This might be my favorite. *(Reading)* "Please number the items in the following list from one to twelve, in order of your willingness to kill them, where one is 'most acceptable' and twelve is 'least acceptable.' A pig. A puppy. A roach. A cow. A horsefly. A horse. A dragonfly. A dragon. A baby. A lobster. A celebrity. A stranger."

NICHOLAS: I don't really see what's wrong with that. We have an enormous sample set; we're already asking questions; why not use them as a resource? Get some real answers. It's important to me, Pete.

PETE: Well, glad to see Little Nicky lookin' out for numero one, but guess what, bro? *It's not important to the census bureau.* Not on their time and not on their dime. Hey, d'ja hear that? Maybe I should skip this statistics shit and become Poet Fucking Laureate. 'Cause you know, that would be important to *me*.

NICHOLAS: Pete —

PETE: No, and two? You're upsetting people. We got complaints from nearly every district about this, people saying they're not gonna return any of the forms, claiming mental aggravation —

NICHOLAS: Because I'm making them think? Asking them to step back for one moment, and consider their personal ethos —

PETE: No, you schmuck, it's because you're asking them to KILL things. For sixteen fucking pages!

NICHOLAS: But it's not about killing. It's qualitative analysis, and it's about *keeping*. What makes something worth the effort. Is it better if it's antique? Expensive? Beautiful? Historic? If it provides sustenance? If you're homeless, would you chop down a two-hundred-year-old tree to build shelter? If you're freezing, would you use it for firewood? Or other things — rare books? Is anything flammable fair game? What if you're not freezing — what if you're just cold? Is it worth it to warm your hands briefly over the Gutenberg Bible? Or how about just a bunch of blank paper? What if you didn't realize that that blank paper was about to contain the next Great American Novel?

PETE: Dude.

All we want to know is race, gender, income, dependents, how far do you fucking commute to work? You want to "figure something out" about people's ethos . . . es? Fine! Go. Take some time off, but don't accost an entire city!

Seriously. Toolshed. What is *wrong* with you? This is a fireable offense I gotta cover up here, plus you're slacking on the job, don't think I'm the only one who's noticed, reading fucking psychology books —

NICHOLAS: Philosophy.

PETE: And top it all off, Ma's still calling me, trying to reach you, says you dropped off the face of the earth, she's worried you're dead or worse, and I can't help thinking: Is this my fault? Was I that camel who gave my brother a straw to sip from, and then broke his back? 'Cause I gotta say, I'm doubting my choice to give you that presentation now. And I don't like being doubted. Particularly by myself.

NICHOLAS: No. Pete. You're not — You're not wrong about me. I can do the presentation.

PETE: Yeah, but why would I still LET you?

(Pause.)

NICHOLAS: Right.

PETE: Fuck yeah, I'm right.

(Pause. Staredown.)

Remove the supplementals. All of them. Call anyone who received one. Alert them that there's been a prank. A *prank*. We don't know by who; we're gonna find out. Apologize. I'm talking profuse. Use some of your big philosophy words.

Stop reading philosophy at work.

Call Ma.

(Pete looks at his watch.)

FYI, this little convo took us five minutes, easy. Did I say "sixty seconds"? Yes, I did. What I did *not* say was "sixty seconds *or more*."

(Pete looks for something to hit, to release pent-up anger. Settles on the cubicle wall. He punches it.)

Waste of my life, I swear.

SOUL SAMURAI
Qui Nguyen

Comic
Dewdrop, nineteen
Cert, nineteen

Dewdrop, a down-and-out teenage girl, explains how she first met Cert, a high-energy b-boy (a break dancer), to the audience. Then, we see Cert trying to pick up an uninterested Dewdrop at an abandoned bus stop. (Note: A backslash [/] indicates where the next line of dialogue overlaps the current one.)

DEWDROP: *(To audience.)* Yeah, I was a cliché of self-inflicting pain. I was hurting and I wanted to hurt. I wanted revenge. I knew who to blame for all this — the Longtooths — but had no power in stopping them. *(Lights come up on Cert as he jams out wearing headphones.)*

DEWDROP: *(Voiceover, continued.)*: And that's when I met him . . .

CERT: *(To himself.)* My name is Cert
I'm here to kick it
Don't step to me, boy,
'Cause my shit is wicked
Ninja fly shit is how I be dealin' it
I'm a Samurai, son, so you best be feelin' it

Konichiwa, bozu,
Fuck you up old Schoo'
Knock out ya teeth like a Eastside Sifu

Remember these words
Remember my face
I'm the C. E. R. T.
This hood's my place.

DEWDROP: Hey! Will you shut the fuck up?

CERT: Why hello there, fly girl.

DEWDROP: No, you don't have to come over —

CERT: Yo, baby, did you clean your pants with Windex? Cause I can practically see myself in them.

DEWDROP: That was lame.

CERT: My name? Did you just ask me my name?

DEWDROP: No, I said "That was lame."

CERT: My name is Damon. But my homies call me Cert. \ You can call me anything you want.

DEWDROP: Don't sit by me. OK, now you're sitting by me. Great. You're completely ignoring —

CERT: What's yo' name?

DEWDROP: Fuck off.

CERT: Is that Russian?

DEWDROP: Look, bozu. You should probably go ahead and give up cause I ain't / interested.

CERT: I love Russian chicks.

DEWDROP: Do I look Russian?

CERT: Not traditionally. But I'm black and I ain't exactly dark-complected, now am I? My mom's Jewish. But I'm hung like a brotha if you know what I mean . . .

DEWDROP: No, I certainly don't.

CERT: You wanna go find a place we can go talk in private like?

DEWDROP: Look, I like girls, OK?

CERT: So do I.

DEWDROP: No. I'm a lesbian.

CERT: Well, Cinderella was a bum before she got transformed by her Fairy Godmother.

DEWDROP: Are you my Fairy Godmother now?

CERT: No, but I do got a magic stick! HEY-O!

DEWDROP: That was horrible.

CERT: But it made you crack a smile.

DEWDROP: You stupid.

CERT: I might be stupid, but I ain't the one waiting at a bus stop that hasn't seen a bus in over a year. What?

DEWDROP: Touché.

CERT: So do you wanna —

DEWDROP: No.

CERT: OK. Can I just get your —

DEWDROP: No.

Look, we're not going to hang out, we're not gonna make time, be buds, bump fists, or be homies, not even in the most general sense. I don't like you, OK? This is not going to or ever going to happen, ya dig?

CERT: We'll see.

SOUTHERN RAPTURE

Eric Coble

More information on this playwright may be found in the "Meet Our Authors" tab at www.smithandkraus.com.

Seriocomic
Simon, thirties to forties
Mickey, thirties to forties

Simon is a reporter, interested in stirring up trouble over a local theater's production of Rapture in America *(a doppelgänger for* Angels in America*). Here, he invades the actors' dressing room to confront one of the actors in the play.*

SIMON: Excuse me? Mr. Stedman?

MICKEY: Just a minute

SIMON: Simon Fitzsimmons. With *The Repository*

MICKEY: Oh my God! Hi! Yeah! Hi! Come on in!

SIMON: No need to put on pants on my account.

(Mickey hesitates.)

SIMON: I mean. Of course you can. I don't *not* want you to wear pants.

MICKEY: Right, no, I don't care. Whatever! You know! We're all friends here, right? *(Mickey laughs.)*

SIMON: Absolutely. I just wonder if I can catch a word with you? Is this your dinner break?

MICKEY: *(Sitting again, his pants halfway up.)* No. I mean, yes, technically, but I'm not hungry. *(Holds up a little Tupperware container.)*

MICKEY: I've got carrot sticks. Would you like one?

SIMON: No. Thank you. I loved your work in *Will Rogers' Follies.*

MICKEY: Thank you, it was a great cast, great company, thank you. And it was right after our production of *Amadeus*, so it was quite a shift —

SIMON: Yeah. I didn't care so much for that one.

MICKEY: Me either.

SIMON: But I loved *Will Rogers' Follies.*

MICKEY: And I loved your review of *Will Rogers' Follies.*

SIMON: Very different role now, isn't it?

MICKEY: Less singing and lassoing, yes.

SIMON: More immune-deficiency disorders and guilt-ridden religious hallucinations.

MICKEY: *(Laughs.)* Yes! Yes, exactly! Yes.

(Beat. Mickey sits expectantly.)

SIMON: So is all the furor affecting your performance

MICKEY: What furor?

SIMON: The —

MICKEY: Oh, that, yeah, yeah, no. No. We're all just hunkering down, you know.

(Simon starts writing.)

MICKEY: We're trying to make a family of art, you know, to serve the community with stories that can be scary or happy campfire stories that we tell with grace and happiness. Stories with new things our family may not have heard of, like anal intercourse.

(Simon looks up.)

MICKEY: We're making art

SIMON: *(Jots that down.)* Are you scared?

MICKEY: Of?

SIMON: *(Shrugs.)* Hate mail, death threats, that sort of thing.

MICKEY: No. None of that.

(Beat. Simon writes.)

MICKEY: Why. Have you heard something?

SIMON: Not specifically. There's just some people out there. Angry people. Angry people who own firearms. I think you're very brave.

MICKEY: What, um, what kind of firearms

SIMON: You all planning any security?

MICKEY: . . . I don't know

SIMON: What would you say to these people?

MICKEY: Um.

SIMON: I mean, you must be furious too, right?

MICKEY: . . . I don't know . . .

SIMON: Here they are threatening your art, your very life — I mean you could be acting, saying your lines and BOOM there's a bullet in your jugular and you're writhing on the stage spraying blood because you committed the sin of taking off your clothes! Don't you have anything you'd want to tell these people?

MICKEY: . . . put down the rifle?

SIMON: *(Doesn't write.)* You're a very popular actor in town, Mickey.

MICKEY: Thank you.

SIMON: So I wonder what it does to your career to be a homosexual . . .

(Mickey starts to respond.)

SIMON: onstage.

MICKEY: But I'm not! I mean I am playing one, but I'm *playing* one. I mean not that I'm not not playing one in real life, but that's not the point, I'm an actor!

SIMON: A naked gay actor in the Bible Belt.

MICKEY: No!! I'm pretending! I play a gay man the way I'd play . . . Daddy Warbucks in *Annie*.

SIMON: You think Daddy Warbucks was gay?

MICKEY: NO!! I mean, no, not that I'm not saying he's not gay, I'm saying that it's a role, I'm acting. I'm an actor. I take in orphans and have consensual male intercourse. That's what I have to give to the community.

SIMON: *(Writing furiously, glances up and — smiles.)* Thank you.

THE UNDERSTUDY
Theresa Rebeck

Comic
Harry, thirties
Jake, thirties

Harry is the new understudy for Jake, whose career as an action film star is starting to take off. Harry is a struggling stage actor who resents Jake's film celebrity. During a break in rehearsal, the two dudes bond.

HARRY: You know, I meant what I said. About your acting.

JAKE: Surprised you, huh? The action star can actually pull it out?

HARRY: Well, you know, you can't really tell anything from those movies. In between explosions there's not a lot of room for — subtlety.

JAKE: You're a snob.

HARRY: I'm not a snob. I'm an understudy. Come on, do it.

JAKE: Do what?

HARRY: *(Mouthing.)* "Get in the truck."

JAKE: You want me to do it?

(Harry nods. After a moment —)

JAKE: *(Continued, full out.)* GET IN THE TRUCK!

(It is awesome.)

HARRY: That's good. That is, it's good.

(Jake grins; they both know it's ridiculous and thrilling.)

JAKE: Why are you doing this, man? You're a real actor. Roxanne is right. There's like no chance you'll ever go on. You know that, don't you?

HARRY: I might go on.

JAKE: Dude, you might go on, and the entire audience might ask for their money back.

HARRY: There might be a few people out there who are coming to see a first-rate production of Kafka on Broadway.

JAKE: Yeah, nobody cares about those people. They care about all those other people coming in on buses from New Jersey. And trust me, THOSE people are coming to see me and Bruce.

HARRY: But what if Bruce gets sick and you have to go on for Bruce. Then I would go on for you.

JAKE: Bruce doesn't get sick.

HARRY: He might get sick. Or you might get sick and then I would go on for you.

JAKE: It's Broadway, nobody gets sick.

HARRY: Everybody gets sick.

JAKE: Nobody gets sick on Broadway. People leave shows. Bruce could leave the show, he could get mercury poisoning and leave the show, and then I would go on for him and they would cast some other movie star as me.

HARRY: So you wouldn't be you anymore, you would be Bruce.

JAKE: That's right.

HARRY: But I would still be me. I would still be the understudy.

JAKE: Yeah.

HARRY: So I might go on.

JAKE: You're not going on!

HARRY: I just don't choose to see it that way.

JAKE: Dude, it doesn't matter how you choose to see it.

HARRY: It matters to me.

JAKE: It doesn't matter to anyone else.

HARRY: If it doesn't matter, then I can choose what I want.

JAKE: You can choose what you want, but what you want is not your choice.

HARRY: You sound like Kafka now.

JAKE: Awesome. 'Cause he was really smart.

(Jake takes out a banana from the drawer and then a second, which he hands to Harry.)

JAKE: Don't tell Roxanne. She throws a fit when we eat the props.

HARRY: Bananas. That's right, the banana scene is coming up too.

JAKE: So why are you doing this? I mean basically they just pay you not to act, right? They pay you to learn the part and then just stand by?

HARRY: The operative part of that sentence being "pay me."

JAKE: You need the money.

HARRY: An actor who needs money. Hmmmm. What a unique situation.

JAKE: Right? Right?

(He enjoys this. They eat their bananas.)

HARRY: Is that why you did the get-in-the-truck movie?

JAKE: I love that movie! I did it for artistic fulfillment, man!

(He laughs and eats his banana.)

HARRY: OK, just for curiosity's sake.

JAKE: Uh-huh.

HARRY: Just to make me feel a little nauseous, help me get into character for the rest of the scene —

JAKE: Yeaaahhh.

HARRY: How much.

JAKE: *(Working him.)* How much what.

HARRY: Come on.

JAKE: Two point three. Million.

HARRY: *(Shocked.)* Two point three million what? Pesos?

JAKE: Dollars.

HARRY: Two point three MILLION dollars? That's how much they paid you to make that terrible movie? Two point three million DOLLARS?

JAKE: It's not that much after agents and lawyers and taxes. You know, it doesn't go that far.

HARRY: It doesn't go far? It's millions of dollars! How could that not go far?

JAKE: It just doesn't. Keeping the whole machine going costs a lot of money, it doesn't, you know — honestly I'm kind of a bottom basement movie star. Two point three million? That's actually a pretty lame quote. I kind of got that part because the CGI was going to cost a fortune so they were looking to save money and I was like the cheapest action star out there. Bruce, you want to know what Bruce gets?

HARRY: I don't know, do I?

JAKE: Twenty-two.

HARRY: Million. Twenty-two million DOLLARS? A movie? Like for one movie?

JAKE: Where have you been? Everybody in America knows that's his quote.

HARRY: And it doesn't matter that he's terrible?

JAKE: Dude — you know you can't say that right? Like, what if he was in the theater?

HARRY: Well, I wouldn't say it if he was here. I'm not stupid.

JAKE: Yeah that's still up for debate because let me ask you this: What if he left something in his dressing room? Like his sweatshirt or something, what if he left his favorite sweatshirt, by mistake, in his dressing room, and he stopped by to pick it up.

And he came in through the stage door because he's just going to run in and get it? And he heard you saying this shit over the loudspeakers. What if that happened.

HARRY: He has a favorite sweatshirt? Why doesn't he just buy another one, he makes twenty-two million dollars a movie.

JAKE: You make that much money you don't really buy things anymore.

HARRY: What do you mean you don't "buy" things?

JAKE: Well, I don't have that kind of money so I don't fully understand this from the inside. But you know, you don't "purchase" things. Things move different. When it gets that big, money — works — different. You know this.

HARRY: No I don't.

JAKE: You know, it like, floats. And then you float. It's all about meaning.

HARRY: Meaning?

JAKE: Meaning. Like yes, no. Words. Meaning.

HARRY: What about meaning?

JAKE: That's what I'm saying. The meaning changes.

HARRY: What are we talking about?

JAKE: OK look. Meaning. This is a banana. Only it's not a banana, it's a prop.

HARRY: It's a prop AND a banana.

JAKE: Except to Bruce it's nothing. It doesn't exist. Bananas don't exist for him.

HARRY: Really?

JAKE: No. Guatemala exists, because he could BUY Guatemala, and then the percentage of the gross national product that consists of banana futures in Guatemala, that would exist for him. But this banana? Has no meaning.

HARRY: Do YOU have meaning?

JAKE: What are you talking about. Me? Of course I have meaning.

HARRY: Just not as much meaning.

JAKE: I have meaning!

HARRY: Not as much meaning as you'd have if you made twenty-two million a movie.

JAKE: I have more meaning than you.

HARRY: Oh me, please. I have like negative meaning. What is negative meaning? Can you have negative meaning? If you have negative meaning is it still meaning?

JAKE: You know who would know the answer to this? Kafka.

HARRY: Really, you think so?

JAKE: Have you read the play? That's what the play's about!

HARRY: You know I have to say I have read the play, but I don't understand the play.

JAKE: You don't understand the play?

HARRY: Do you understand the play?

JAKE: Absolutely.

HARRY: What's it about?

JAKE: It's about meaning.

UNUSUAL ACTS OF DEVOTION

Terrence McNally

More information on this playwright may be found in the "Meet Our Authors" tab at www.smithandkraus.com.

Dramatic
Chick, thirties to forties
Leo, thirties to forties

Chick and Leo have gathered on the rooftop of their Greenwich Village apartment building with other residents to celebrate the fifth wedding anniversary of a couple, Leo and Nadine, who also live there. Chick is a gay, alcoholic tour guide. Here, in a moment alone with Leo, he comes on to him.

CHICK: We've got your Edith Piaf, Mrs. Darnell. She was right where I told Leo she was.

(He pronounces Edith the proper French way.)

LEO: I thought her name was Edith?

CHICK: It is, only in France it's pronounced Ay-dee

LEO: Here you go.

(Leo has put some progressive jazz on.)

CHICK: That's not Piaf. That's not anyone. That's not even human.

LEO: I'm going to open you up, Chick. *(Calling.)* Your gal is in the wings, Mrs. Darnell. Mr. Davis is going to do his magic first.

CHICK: I don't want opening up.

LEO: I'm giving you the sublime, Chick. Tell him, Mrs. Darnell! You're an old hipster, right? She must be asleep. You're not listening.

CHICK: I'm listening.

LEO: You don't look like you're listening. Will you tell Nadine if I smoke a cigarette?

CHICK: Of course not. The way this evening's going, I might even join you.

(Leo lights up and smokes.)

LEO: Listen to those intervals. Genius. You could disappear in them.

CHICK: I just don't get it.

LEO: Tell me something, seriously, man to man: when was the last time you got laid, Chick?

CHICK: I'm not going to answer that.

LEO: Why not?

CHICK: I don't want to.

LEO: That's a good reason.

CHICK: It's none of your business.

LEO: That's another one.

CHICK: When is the last time you got laid?

LEO: What's today? Thursday —

CHICK: Never mind! I don't want to know.

LEO: It's what people do. They take physical pleasure in one another.

CHICK: I know that.

LEO: Without that pleasure, they . . . they.

CHICK: They what?

LEO: I don't know. I've never lived without it. You grow up straight in the Village like I did, the world's pretty much your oyster. Of course you grow up gay in the Village, and you could pretty much say the same thing. That was the old days. All you guys are in Chelsea now.

CHICK: 1 know. They left me to hold down the fort.

LEO: Don't try to get me off point, Chick. Without that pleasure, they —

CHICK: Turn into me. Can we change the subject and the music now?

LEO: I didn't say that.

CHICK: Or Josie.

LEO: Tell me that's a happy woman, Chick.

CHICK: Happiness is highly overrated.

LEO: When was the last time someone put their arms around you and held you?

CHICK: I don't remember

LEO: Nay holds me like that all the time. She's always touching me. I'm always touching her

CHICK: Aaron and I had that.

LEO: Aaron's gone.

CHICK: We were so happy.

LEO: You were happy. Aaron took his own life.

(Chick turns back to the music.)

CHICK: I'm sorry, I need a melody.

LEO: You want stories, explanations where there are none.

(Chick turns off the music.)

CHICK: Have you ever been intimate with a man?

LEO: I thought I was being intimate with one right now.

CHICK: You know what I mean.

LEO: I can't believe you put it like that. What is this? Bible class? Yes, I have been intimate with a man. You want details?

CHICK: Yes. No. I don't know. I thought you'd say "no, never," even if you had.

LEO: How long have you waited to ask me that question?

CHICK: When did I first meet you?

LEO: Actually, I've slept with more than one man . . .

CHICK: I can't believe this.

LEO: Four, I think.

CHICK: You think?

LEO: No, four.

CHICK: When was this?

LEO: At various intervals in my life. Not last night, if that's what you're thinking. High school, on the road once, stuff like that.

CHICK: What are the possibilities of making it five?

LEO: Remote, but I never say never, you know? Life happens.

CHICK: I meant with me.

LEO: I know you did.

CHICK: I bet I could make you happy, Leo. And I don't mean for five minutes right now. I mean happy for a long time, the long haul kind of happy.

LEO: No, you couldn't, Chick, and that's the tragedy of life.

CHICK: No, that's the tragedy of my life.

LEO: That's the tragedy of everybody's life.

CHICK: And you're straight.

LEO: Yes, I'm straight.

CHICK: Except for four men. The Beginner's Luck Four!

LEO: Why do you always have to make a joke?

CHICK: I honestly think I should have been one of them.

LEO: I asked you a question.

CHICK: So I don't get a gun and blow somebody's head off. So I don't drive the bus into the Hudson and drown forty uncomprehending foreigners. So I don't follow Aaron over that parapet. *(Pause.)* I'll put your Miles back on. Anything is better than this.

(Music resumes.)

LEO: Did you really sleep with —

CHICK: Josie? She's pretty upset I —

LEO: I did, too. I slept with her right after I got married.

CHICK: I know. She told me.

LEO: That bitch. And I mean that affectionately. I like Josie.

CHICK: She didn't exactly tell me, she let me surmise.

LEO: She's probably down there right now letting Nadine surmise.

CHICK: Josie wouldn't do that.

LEO: Nadine knows. I told her. Let sleeping dogs lie. That's a lousy metaphor. None of us are dogs. We try to do the right thing and end up doing absolutely the opposite.

(Silence. Pause.)

CHICK: Would you dance with me if I asked you?

LEO: Sure.

CHICK: You would?

LEO: What's the matter?

CHICK: You were supposed to say no.

LEO: Life's too short for that shit: Supposed to this, supposed to that. Who makes that shit up?

(Dance music with a good beat fills the night. Leo makes a space for them to dance, then goes to Chick and stands very close to him.)

LEO: Be gentle with me, Chick, I've never danced with a man before. Who's gonna lead?

CHICK: Well, I'm certainly not.

(They start to dance. They look surprisingly good together surprisingly quickly.)

CHICK: You're good.

LEO: Thank you. So are you.

CHICK: Thank you.

LEO: I guess you did this with Aaron.

CHICK: He didn't like to dance.

LEO: Maybe he didn't know how.

CHICK: He never wanted to.

LEO: He could have taken lessons.

CHICK: I tried to teach him. It wasn't natural to him. Josie was the dancer in the family. *(Calling off to a neighboring apartment house.)* What are you looking at? You never saw two men dancing together before? Go back to Cleveland!

LEO: That's telling 'em.

CHICK: Let's hope they don't come up here!

LEO: Let 'em try. I'll take care of them.

CHICK: I know you would.

LEO: I'm pretty good that way; I'm a New Yorker. You're from New Jersey. You should be pretty good that way, too.

CHICK: I'm not from that part of New Jersey.

CHICK: Are you trying to seduce me, Leo?

LEO: No way!

CHICK: Then why are you dancing like you're trying to seduce me?

LEO: I'm Italian. It's how we dance. What are you?

CHICK: Gay. It's how we dance, too.

LEO: Not every dance is a seduction, Chick.

LEO: It's just a dance

CHICK: That's either very profound or very stupid.

LEO: It's the truth.

CHICK: I hate that word.

LEO: No, you hate the concept.

CHICK: Only in New York would I be dancing on a roof with a straight man on his wedding anniversary.

(Leo stops dancing and looks at Chick.)

LEO: Marry Josie, Chick

CHICK: Marry Josie? Where did that come from?

LEO: Take care of each other while there's still time to.

CHICK: When I asked you if we should, you said "that's nuts."

LEO: That was a lifetime ago. A lot's happened since then. Think about it, just think. Will you do that, Chick?

CHICK: There isn't a day that I don — *(Chick stops dancing.)* Has this whole evening been a setup?

LEO: No way, Chick. Nadine and I are not that kind of cunning people. We're fucking quasi-hippies. This is completely spontaneous, like dancing with you is.

(He is leading Chick back into dancing with him again.)

Swinging and swaying with our across-the-hall neighbor and telling him to allow some love in his life was the last thing I had in mind when we came up here tonight.

Rights and Permissions

IMPORTANT NOTE: The complete text of every play in this volume is available from the performance rights holder, except as otherwise noted.

MONOLOGUES

AMERICAN WHUP-ASS © 2007 by Justin Warner. Reprinted by permission of the author. For performance rights, contact Original Works (www.originalworksonline.com/americanwhup-ass.htm).

CELL © 2009 by Judy Klass. Reprinted by permission of the author. For performance rights, contact Samuel French, 45 W. 25th St., New York, NY 10010 (www.samuelfrench.com) (212-206-8990).

DEFENDER OF THE FAITH © 2008 by Stuart Carolan. Reprinted by permission of Curtis Brown, London. For performance rights, contact Dramatists Play Service, 440 Park Ave. S., New York, NY 10016 (www.dramatists.com) (212-683-8960).

DRIVING GREEN © 2009 by Martin Blank. Reprinted by permission of the author. For performance rights, contact Pat McLaughlin, Beacon Artists Agency (beaconagency@hotmail.com). The entire text of this play is published by Smith and Kraus in *The Best Ten-Minute Plays 2010*.

EMILIE'S VOLTAIRE © 2008 by Arthur Giron. Reprinted by permission of Barbara Hogenson. For performance rights, contact Samuel French, 45 W. 25th St., New York, NY 10010 (www.samuelfrench.com) (212-206-8990).

EMOTION MEMORY © 2009 by Don Nigro. Reprinted by permission of the author. For performance rights, contact Samuel French, 45 W. 25th St., New York, NY 10010 (www.samuelfrench.com) (212-206-8990).

FARRAGUT NORTH © 2008 by Beau Willimon. Reprinted by permission of Chris Till, Creative Artists Agency. For performance rights, contact Dramatists Play Service, 440 Park Ave. S., New York, NY 10016 (www.dramatists.com) (212-683-8960).

FROST/NIXON © 2009 by Peter Morgan. Reprinted by permission of Victoria Fox, Faber and Faber. For performance rights, contact Dramatists Play Service, 440 Park Ave. S., New York, NY 10016 (www.dramatists.com) (212-683-8960).

THE GINGERBREAD HOUSE © 2009 by Mark Schultz. Reprinted by permission of Olivier Sultan, Creative Artists Agency. For performance rights, contact Dramatists Play Service, 440 Park Ave. S., New York, NY 10016 (www.dramatists.com) (212-683-8960).

THE GOOD NEGRO © 2008 by Tracey Scott Wilson. Reprinted by permission of Morgan Jenness, Abrams Artists Agency. For performance rights, contact Dramatists Play Service, 440 Park Ave. S., New York, NY 10016 (www.dramatists.com) (212-683-8960).

GROUND © 2010 by Lisa Dillman. Reprinted by permission of Selma Luttinger, Robert Freedman Dramatic Agency. For performance rights, contact Selma Luttinger (sl@bromasite.com).

GUINEA PIG SOLO © 2009 by Brett C. Leonard. Reprinted by permission of the author. For performance rights, contact Broadway Play Publishing, 56 E. 81st St., New York, NY 10021 (www.broadwayplaypubl.com) (212-772-8334).

A HUMAN INTEREST STORY (OR THE GORY DETAILS AND ALL) © 2008 by Carlos Murillo. Reprinted by permission of Antje Oegel, AO International. For performance rights, contact Antje Oegel (aoegel@aoegelinternational.com). The entire text of this play is published by Smith and Kraus in *The Best Ten-Minute Plays 2010.*

IN THE SAWTOOTHS © 2009 by Dano Madden. Reprinted by permission of the author. For performance rights, contact Samuel French, 45 W. 25th St., New York, NY 10010 (www.samuelfrench.com) (212-206-8990).

LOST GENERATION © 2008 by Don Nigro. Reprinted by permission of the author. For performance rights, contact Samuel French, 45 W. 25th St., New York, NY 10010 (www.samuelfrench.com) (212-206-8990).

MAHIDA'S EXTRA KEY TO HEAVEN © 2009 by Russell Davis. Reprinted by permission of Susan Gurman. For performance rights, contact Susan Gurman (susan@gurmanagency.com).

MEATBALL HERO © 2009 by Richard Vetere. Reprinted by permission of the author. For performance rights, contact Smith and Kraus (www.smithandkraus.com). The entire text of this play is published by Smith and Kraus in *The Best Ten-Minute Plays 2010.*

MISTAKES WERE MADE © 2009 by Craig Wright. Reprinted by permission of Beth Blickers, Abrams Artists Agency. For performance rights, contact Beth Blickers (beth.blickers@abramsartny.com).

NEW JERUSALEM © 2009 by David Ives. Reprinted by permission of Peter Hagan, Abrams Artists Agency. For performance rights, contact Dramatists Play Service, 440 Park Ave. S., New York, NY 10016 (www.dramatists.com) (212-683-8960).

NEXT FALL © 2009 by Geoffrey Nauffts. Reprinted by permission of Olivier Sultan, Creative Artists Agency. For performance rights, contact Olivier Sultan (osultan@caa.com).

9 CIRCLES © 2009 by Bill Cain. Reprinted by permission of Beth Blickers, Abrams Artists Agency. For performance rights, contact Beth Blickers (beth.blickers@abramsartny.com)

THE OPTIMIST © 2009 by Jason Chimonides. Reprinted by permission of Pouya Shahbazian, Mandown Pictures & Management. For performance rights, contact Dramatists Play Service, 440 Park Ave. S., New York, NY 10016 (www.dramatists.com) (212-683-8960).

OUR HOUSE © 2009 by Madwoman in the Attic, Inc.. Reprinted by permission of Theresa Rebeck. For performance rights, contact Samuel French, 45 W. 25th St., New York, NY 10010 (www.samuelfrench.com) (212-206-8990).

PARASITE DRAG © 2009 by Mark Roberts. Reprinted by permission of Chris Till, Creative Artists Agency. For performance rights, contact Dramatists Play Service, 440 Park Ave. S., New York, NY 10016 (www.dramatists.com) (212-683-8960).

PRAYER FOR MY ENEMY © 2007 by Craig Lucas. Reprinted by permission of Jonathan Lomma, William Morris Endeavor Entertainment. For performance rights, contact Samuel French, 45 W. 25th St., New York, NY 10010 (www.samuelfrench.com) (212-206-8990).

PUSSY BOY © 2002 by Christine Evans. Reprinted by permission of Peregrine Whittlesey. For performance rights, contact Peregrine Whittlesey (pwwagy@aol.com)

RAVISHED © 2009 by Don Nigro. Reprinted by permission of the author. For performance rights, contact Samuel French, 45 W. 25th St., New York, NY 10010 (www.samuelfrench.com) (212-206-8990).

REENTRY © 2010 by Emily Ackerman and KJ Sanchez. Reprinted by permission of the authors. For performance rights, contact Emily Ackerman (emilyackerman@yahoo.com) and KJ Sanchez (kjsanchez@trtc.org).

THE REST OF THE NIGHT © 2009 by Robert Lewis Vaughan. Reprinted by permission of the author. For performance rights, contact Dramatists Play Service, 440 Park Ave. S., New York, NY 10016 (www.dramatists.com) (212-683-8960).

ROCKET CITY, ALABAM' © 2009 by Mark Saltzman. Reprinted by permission of the author. For performance rights, contact Samuel French, 45 W. 25th St., New York, NY 10010 (www.samuelfrench.com) (212-206-8990).

THE ROOKY WOOD © 2009 by Don Nigro. Reprinted by permission of the author. For performance rights, contact Samuel French, 45 W. 25th St., New York, NY 10010 (www.samuelfrench.com) (212-206-8990).

ROUGH SKETCH © 2007 by Shawn Nacol. Reprinted by permission of the author. For performance rights, contact Ron Gwiazda, Abrams Artists Agency (ron.gwiazda@abramsartny.com).

SLIPPING © 2009 by Daniel Talbott. Reprinted by permission of Morgan Jenness, Abrams Artists Agency. For performance rights, contact Dramatists Play Service, 440 Park Ave. S., New York, NY 10016 (www.dramatists.com) (212-683-8960).

SMUDGE © 2010 by Rachel Axler. Reprinted by permission of Mark Subias. For performance rights, contact Samuel French, 45 W. 25th St., New York, NY 10010 (www.samuelfrench.com) (212-206-8990).

SOUTHERN RAPTURE © 2008 by Eric Coble. Reprinted by permission of Jonathan Lomma, William Morris Endeavor Entertainment. For performance rights, contact Jonathan Lomma (jxl@wmeentertainment.com).

SUICIDE, INCORPORATED © 2008 by Andrew Hinderaker. Reprinted by permission of the author. For performance rights, contact Andrew Hinderaker (andrewhinderaker@yahoo.com).

THAT PRETTY PRETTY; OR, THE RAPE PLAY © 2009 by Sheila Callaghan. Reprinted by permission of Seth Glewen, The Gersh Agency. For performance rights, contact Samuel French, 45 W. 25th St., New York, NY 10010 (www.samuelfrench.com) (212-206-8990).

THE THIRD STORY © 2008 by Charles Busch. Reprinted by permission of Olivier Sultan, Creative Artists Agency. For performance rights, contact Samuel French, 45 W. 25th St., New York, NY 10010 (www.samuelfrench.com) (212-206-8990).

TROJAN BARBIE © 2007 by Christine Evans. Reprinted by permission of Peregrine Whittlesey. For performance rights, contact Samuel French, 45 W. 25th St., New York, NY 10010 (www.samuelfrench.com) (212-206-8990).

THE UNDERSTUDY © 2009 by Madwoman in the Attic, Inc.. Reprinted by permission of Theresa Rebeck. For performance rights, contact Samuel French, 45 W. 25th St., New York, NY 10010 (www.samuelfrench.com) (212-206-8990).

THE UNSEEN. © by Craig Wright. Reprinted by permission of Beth Blickers, Abrams Artists Agency. For performance rights, contact Beth Blickers (beth.blickers@abramsartny.com).

UNUSUAL ACTS OF DEVOTION © 2009 by Terrence McNally. Reprinted by permission of Jonathan Lomma, William Morris Endeavor Entertainment. For performance rights, contact Jonathan Lomma (jxl@wmeentertainment.com).

Scenes

CREATURE © 2009 by Heidi Schreck. Reprinted by permission of Morgan Jenness, Abrams Artists Agency. For performance rights, contact Morgan Jenness (morgan.jenness@abramsartny.com).

DREAMTIME. © 2008 by Maura Campbell. Reprinted by permission of the author. For performance rights, contact Maura Campbell (ibsen3000@yahoo.com).

FARRAGUT NORTH © 2008 by Beau Willimon. Reprinted by permission of Chris Till, Creative Artists Agency. For performance rights, contact Dramatists Play Service, 440 Park Ave. S., New York, NY 10016 (www.dramatists.com) (212-683-8960).

THE GOOD NEGRO © 2008 by Tracey Scott Wilson. Reprinted by permission of Morgan Jenness, Abrams Artists Agency. For performance rights, contact Dramatists Play Service, 440 Park Ave. S., New York, NY 10016 (www.dramatists.com) (212-683-8960).

LIONS © 2009 Vince Melocchi. Reprinted by permission of Chris Till, Creative Artists Agency. For performance rights, contact Samuel French, 45 W. 25th St., New York, NY 10010 (www.samuelfrench.com) (212-206-8990).

NEXT FALL © 2009 by Geoffrey Nauffts. Reprinted by permission of Olivier Sultan, Creative Artists Agency. For performance rights, contact Olivier Sultan (osultan@caa.com).

OUR HOUSE © 2009 by Madwoman in the Attic, Inc.. Reprinted by permission of Theresa Rebeck. For performance rights, contact Samuel French, 45 W. 25th St., New York, NY 10010 (www.samuelfrench.com) (212-206-8990).

PARASITE DRAG © 2009 by Mark Roberts. Reprinted by permission of Chris Till, Creative Artists Agency. For performance rights, contact Dramatists Play Service, 440 Park Ave. S., New York, NY 10016 (www.dramatists.com) (212-683-8960).

ROCKET CITY, ALABAM' © 2009 by Mark Saltzman. Reprinted by permission of the author. For performance rights, contact Samuel French,

45 W. 25th St., New York, NY 10010 (www.samuelfrench.com) (212-206-8990).

THE SECRET LIFE OF SEAGULLS © 2009 by Henry Meyerson. Reprinted by permission of the author. For performance rights, contact Samuel French, 45 W. 25th St., New York, NY 10010 (www.samuelfrench.com) (212-206-8990).

SLIPPING © 2009 by Daniel Talbot. Reprinted by permission of Morgan Jenness, Abrams Artists Agency. For performance rights, contact Dramatists Play Service, 440 Park Ave. S., New York, NY 10016 (www.dramatists.com) (212-683-8960).

SLOW FALLING BIRD © 2004 by Christine Evans. Reprinted by permission of Peregrine Whittlesey. For performance rights, contact Peregrine Whittlesey (pwwagy@aol.com).

SMUDGE © 2010 by Rachel Axler. Reprinted by permission of Mark Subias. For performance rights, contact Samuel French, 45 W. 25th St., New York, NY 10010 (www.samuelfrench.com) (212-206-8990).

SOUL SAMURAI. © 2009 by Qui Nguyen. Reprinted by permission of Bruce Ostler, Bret Adams Ltd. For performance rights, contact Broadway Play Publishing, 56 E. 81st St., New York, NY 10021 (www.broadwayplaypubl.com) (212-772-8334).

SOUTHERN RAPTURE © 2008 by Eric Coble. Reprinted by permission of Jonathan Lomma, William Morris Endeavor Entertainment. For performance rights, contact Jonathan Lomma (jxl@wmeentertainment.com).

THE UNDERSTUDY © 2009 by Madwoman in the Attic, Inc. Reprinted by permission of Theresa Rebeck. For performance rights, contact Samuel French, 45 W. 25th St., New York, NY 10010 (www.samuelfrench.com) (212-206-8990).

UNUSUAL ACTS OF DEVOTION © 2009 by Terrence McNally. Reprinted by permission of Jonathan Lomma, William Morris Endeavor Entertainment. For performance rights, contact Jonathan Lomma (jxl@wmeentertainment.com).